To a good friend,
Bro. Markham

With deep regards,

~ Bill Fisher

WHY
I AM
A
NAZARENE

*and NOT—*a Mormon

a Roman Catholic

a Jehovah's Witness

a Christian Scientist

a Seventh-Day Adventist

WHY
I AM
A
NAZARENE

and **NOT—** a Mormon

a Roman Catholic

a Jehovah's Witness

a Christian Scientist

a Seventh-Day Adventist

C. William Fisher

Nazarene Publishing House
Kansas City, Missouri

EIGHTH PRINTING, 1962

Printed in the United States of America

To my sons
BYRON AND BILLY
with the prayerful hope
that they will never be ensnared
by the delusions of a false faith
but will ever be enriched by the
challenging dimensions of the
faith once delivered unto
the saints.

By the same author

THE TIME IS NOW
SECOND-HAND RELIGION
WAKE UP AND LIFT
OUR HERITAGE AND OUR HOPE

Preface

This is not an exposé.

This is not an attack.

This is, rather, an honest and positive effort towards a fuller understanding of some of the more dangerous distortions of religious beliefs that today confuse and pervert the minds of millions across America and around the world.

Many observations and convictions have made this a compelling task: the clever camouflaging of heresy by the use of a respectable and orthodox vocabulary . . . the deceitful blurring of doctrinal distinctions by those who seek to ensnare . . . the appalling lack of knowledge on the part of Christians concerning the origins and beliefs of the cults . . . the deepening conviction that the light and truth of holiness are more readily seen and more deeply appreciated when held up against the darkness of distortion and delusion.

In times of moderation and easy tolerance it is especially important for one to be able to calmly and knowingly say, "I am THIS, and not THAT"—and to say it without the loud and strident pride that springs from insecurity and doubt, but with the humble and quiet gratitude that flows from assurance and certainty.

Ridicule never reforms. Sarcasm never saves. Disparagement never delivers from delusion. If deliverance and direction are to come, there must not only be close scrutiny of the beliefs; there must be Christian charity toward the believers.

There is no one, of course, who does not believe. As Dr. Buttrick writes: "People are born to believe. They cannot live on questionings. For a man to say in honesty, 'I do not believe that dogma,' may be a virtue, provided he can add with radiant mind, 'Yet I do believe this . . .' But without some positive avowal his negatives become only darkness, for belief is as native as breathing."[1]

Whittaker Chambers speaks with the same accent when he says, "A man is not primarily a witness *against* something. That is only incidental to the fact that he is a witness *for* something."[2]

It is in the spirit of that insight that these pages are written. The detours and deviations of religious belief are examined only that those who find them attractive may be warned and that those who are already diverted may be pointed back to Him who said, "I am the way, the truth, and the life."

If this book creates or intensifies a denominational pride or arrogance, it will have failed its purpose. If it creates or enlarges a charitable understanding of those whose minds are distorted, while at the same time it holds the distortions up to the revealing light of "Thus saith the Lord," and gives to all who read a deeper compassion to lead those who are deceived into the paths of righteousness and true faith, it will prove of the Spirit's doing. And in that measure, and only in that measure, will this book prove profitable to those who read it, and pleasing to Him in whose name it was undertaken.

C. WILLIAM FISHER

God has given you a certain amount of spiritual insight, and indeed I have not written this warning as if I were writing to men who don't know what error is. I write because your eyes are clear enough to discern a lie when you come across it.

I John 2:21 (Phillips)

Acknowledgments

The following publishers have kindly granted permission to quote from their publications:

Abingdon Press, Nashville, Tennessee: *So We Believe, So We Pray*, George A. Buttrick, 1951; and *Handbook of Denominations in the United States*, Frank S. Mead.

Association Press, New York, New York: *Primer for Protestants*, James Hastings Nichols, 1949.

Bobbs-Merrill Company, Indianapolis, Indiana: *They Have Found a Faith*, Marcus Bach, 1946.

Church of Jesus Christ of the Latter-day Saints, Salt Lake City, Utah: *The Articles of Faith*, James E. Talmage, 1952.

Columbia University Press, New York, New York: *The Jehovah's Witnesses*, H. H. Stroup, 1945.

Concordia Publishing House, St. Louis, Missouri: *The Religious Bodies of America*, F. E. Mayer, 1954.

Deseret News Press, Salt Lake City, Utah: *The Way to Perfection*, Joseph Fielding Smith, 1953.

William B. Eerdmans Publishing Company, Grand Rapids, Michigan: *Mormonism Under the Searchlight*, W. E. Biederwolf, 1956; and *Christian Science*, William Edward Biederwolf, 1955.

Guardians of the Faith, Minneapolis, Minnesota: *Why You Should Not Be a Seventh-Day Adventist*, E. B. Jones, 1949.

Harper and Brothers, New York, New York: *What Americans Believe and How They Worship*, J. Paul Williams, 1952. Also, *The New Testament: A New Translation*, by James Moffatt, copyright by Harper and Brothers, 1922, 1935, and 1950.

P. J. Kennedy, New York, New York: *The Faith of Our Fathers*, James Cardinal Gibbons, 1917.

Loizeaux Brothers, Inc., New York, New York: *Heresies Exposed*, W. C. Irvine, 1956; and *Ins and Outs of Romanism*, Joseph Zacchello, 1956.

Macmillan Company, New York, New York: *These Also Believe*, Charles S. Braden, 1949. Also, *Letters to Young Churches*, by J. B. Phillips, copyright by Macmillan, 1947, 1957.

W. W. Norton and Company, Inc., New York, New York: *American Faith*, Ernest Sutherland Bates, 1940.

Philosophical Library, Inc., New York, New York: *Christian Deviations*, Horton Davies, 1954; and *The American Church*, Vergilius Ferm, 1953.

Random House, New York, New York: *Witness*, Whittaker Chambers, 1952.

Scripture Press, Wheaton, Illinois: *How to Win Souls*, Eugene Myers Harrison, 1952.

Simon and Schuster, New York, New York: *A Guide to the Religions of America*, Leo Rosten, 1955.

Southern Methodist University Press, Dallas, Texas: *American Culture and Religion*, William W. Sweet, 1951.

Vantage Press, New York, New York: *Jehovah's Witnesses*, Marley Cole, 1955.

Watchtower Bible and Tract Society, Brooklyn, New York: *The Harp of God*, Rutherford; *The Time Is at Hand*, Vol. II, Russell; *Riches*, Rutherford; *Hell, What Is It?* Russell; *Creation*, Rutherford; *Theocracy*, Rutherford; *Deliverance*, Rutherford; *The Divine Plan of the Ages*, Vol. I, Russell; *Studies in the Scriptures*, Vols. I, II, V, Russell; *Religion Reaps the Whirlwind*, Russell; *Let God Be True*, Russell; *Reconciliation*, Russell; the *Watchtower* issues of October 1, 1931, and September 15, 1910.

Zondervan Publishing House, Grand Rapids, Michigan: *Jehovah of the Watchtower*, Walter R. Martin and Norman H. Klann, 1956.

Contents

| Chapter One | WHY I AM A NAZARENE |

The fact that I state why I am a Nazarene is neither an argument nor an apology. It is, rather, an explanation. An explanation that, in my case, has two parts: why I WAS a Nazarene, and second, why I AM a Nazarene. And, unfortunately, "am" does not always follow "was."

I "was" a Nazarene by inheritance. My parents were Nazarenes when I was born, and my earliest religious recollections are those connected with the Church of the Nazarene—its services, its standards, its revivals, its activities. That these experiences and forces conditioned to a certain extent is not denied. For no one is ever totally independent of his origins.

I "am" a Nazarene, however, by choice—a choice that is continually confirmed and vindicated and verified in countless experiences and observations and changing situations.

Those confirmations come from many sources and they come continually and on every level of life. The church's statement as to what man is and why, and what he may become and how, becomes increasingly valid and satisfying as other statements are studied and found inadequate. The church's disciplines are increasingly understood and appreciated as the heart is hurt and haunted by the tragedy of those lives lived without restraints. Friendships made within the church prove increasingly enriching and rewarding. The inspiration of challenging leadership is increasingly appreciated. The doors of service are repeatedly seen to be as wide open as ability and devotion demand.

Because of all these reasons, and more, I am a Nazarene—and, "I am debtor."

If there is one compelling reason, however, why I choose to be a Nazarene and why that choice is continually confirmed and verified it is that HOLINESS EVANGELISM has been, and is, *the message* and *the mission* of the Church of the Nazarene. All else is secondary and subservient to *that*. All else finds its importance in its relation to *that*. And without *that*, the Church of the Nazarene is just another denomination cluttering the denominational landscape.

Jesus Christ gave His Church one, and only one, mission in the world and that mission was a redemptive one. If the Church fails in that central mission, it has failed Christ, it has failed sinful men, and it has failed its own highest purpose. No success in the secondaries, regardless of how glittering, can ever compensate for the Church's failure in its redemptive mission in the world.

With HOLINESS EVANGELISM at the center, each point and segment on the circumference is but an expression and outreach of that central dynamic. Doctrines and disciplines are but radiations of that central theme. A static holiness—a holiness without outreach—is a contradiction. And evangelism without doctrinal and ethical foundation is sheer enthusiasm. A center without a circumference is as unthinkable as a circumference without a center.

In HOLINESS EVANGELISM, then, the Church of the Nazarene has a center which is fixed, and a circumference which, true to Christ's command, is constantly expanding.

Since the disciplines or ethical demands in most of the groups represented in this study are rather rigid and uniformly high, the basic reason for being a Nazarene and not something else must be found elsewhere.

Doctrine, then, must be the decisive and determining factor in enabling one to say, "I am *this,* and not *that*"— and to say it knowingly, gratefully, and in Christian charity.

What does the Church of the Nazarene say—

1. About Christ?
2. About the Bible?
3. About salvation?
4. About the future life?

These four questions will be asked of each group in this study, and as their answers are given may the Holy Spirit, in love and tender direction, reveal wherein those answers are merely human replies and wherein they are expressions of God's eternal truth.

The clearest and most concise statement as to what Nazarenes believe about these four crucial questions is found in the *Manual* of the Church of the Nazarene. The following quotations are taken from the 1956 edition.

I. WHAT DO NAZARENES BELIEVE ABOUT CHRIST?

We believe in Jesus Christ, the Second Person of the Triune Godhead; that He was eternally one with the Father; that He became incarnate by the Holy Spirit and was born of the Virgin Mary, so that two whole and perfect natures, that is to say the Godhead and manhood, are thus united in one person very God and very man, the God-man.

We believe that Jesus Christ died for our sins, and that He truly arose from the dead and took again His body, together with all things appertaining to the perfection of man's nature, wherewith He ascended into heaven and is there engaged in intercession for us.[1]

We believe that the Lord Jesus Christ will come again; that we who are alive at His coming shall not precede them that are asleep in Christ Jesus; but that, if we are abiding in Him, we shall be caught up with the risen saints to meet the Lord in the air, so that we shall ever be with the Lord.[2]

These are not weasel words. There is no slippery equivocation here. Either Jesus Christ is God-Man or He isn't; Nazarenes believe that He is. Either Jesus Christ died to redeem all men or He didn't; Nazarenes believe that He did. Either Jesus Christ arose from the grave or He didn't; Nazarenes believe that He did. Either Jesus Christ will personally return to this earth or He won't. Nazarenes believe that He will. And in so believing, Nazarenes try to live in such loving relationship with Christ that *whenever* He comes they will be ready to meet Him.

II. WHAT DO NAZARENES BELIEVE ABOUT THE BIBLE?

To all who compose the membership of the Church of the Nazarene, the Bible is the Book of books. It is the Word of God. It "contains all truth necessary to faith and Christian living." It is the "revelation of the will of God concerning us in all things necessary to our salvation." The knowledge and understanding of its teachings, with conformity thereto, is the first duty of all who profess faith in Christ.[3]

We believe in the plenary inspiration of the Holy Scriptures, by which we understand the sixty-six books of the Old and New Testaments given by divine inspiration, inerrantly revealing the will of God concerning us in all things necessary to our salvation, so that whatever is not contained therein is not to be enjoined as an article of faith.[4]

Either the Bible is the inspired Word of God or it isn't; Nazarenes believe that it is. Either the Bible contains all the revelation necessary to salvation or it doesn't; Nazarenes believe that it does. And in so believing they find that, interpreted by the Holy Spirit, the Bible speaks to them of God's will, of God's demands, and of God's loving care.

III. WHAT DO NAZARENES BELIEVE ABOUT SALVATION?

We believe that original sin, or depravity, is the corruption of the nature of all the offspring of Adam by reason of which every one is very far gone from original right-eousness or the pure state of our first parents at the time of their creation, is averse to God, is without spiritual life, and inclined to evil, and that continually. We further believe that original sin continues to exist with the new life of the regenerate, until eradicated by the baptism with the Holy Spirit.

We believe that Jesus Christ, by His sufferings, by the shedding of His own blood, and by His meritorious death on the cross, made a full atonement for all human sin, and that this atonement is the only ground of salvation, and that it is sufficient for every individual of Adam's race. The atonement is graciously efficacious for the salvation of the irresponsible and for the children in innocency, but is efficacious for the salvation of those who reach the age of responsibility only when they repent and believe.[5]

We believe that repentance, which is a sincere and thorough change of the mind in regard to sin, involving a sense of personal guilt and a voluntary turning away from sin, is demanded of all who have by act or purpose become sinners against God. The Spirit of God gives to all who will repent the gracious help of penitence of heart and hope of mercy, that they may believe unto pardon and spiritual life.[6]

We believe that justification, regeneration, and adoption are simultaneous in the experience of seekers after God and are obtained upon the condition of faith, preceded by repentance; and that to this work and state of grace the Holy Spirit bears witness.[7]

We believe that entire sanctification is that act of God, subsequent to regeneration, by which believers are made free from original sin, or depravity, and brought into a state of entire devotement to God, and the holy obedience of love made perfect. It is wrought by the baptism with the Holy Spirit, and comprehends in one experience the cleansing of the heart from sin and the abiding indwelling presence of the Holy Spirit, empowering the believer for life and service.

Entire sanctification is provided by the blood of Jesus, is wrought instantaneously by faith, preceded by entire consecration; and to this work and state of grace the Holy Spirit bears witness. This experience is also known by various terms representing its different phases, such as "Christian Perfection," "Perfect Love," "Heart Purity,"

"The Baptism with the Holy Spirit," "The Fullness of the Blessing," and "Christian Holiness."[8]

Salvation is either by faith or by works; Nazarenes believe that it is by faith—faith in the atoning blood of Christ—and that good works evidence effectual faith. Jesus Christ can either save the sinner from his sins or He can't; Nazarenes believe that He can. Either Jesus Christ can cleanse the believer's heart from all sin or He can't; Nazarenes believe that He can. Either God has provided a way of holiness or He hasn't; Nazarenes believe that He has—and many of them are doing their sincere best to walk that way, living lives of devotement, of surrender, of sacrifice, of obedience; believing, as they do so, that "the blood of Jesus Christ his Son cleanseth us from all sin."

IV. What Do Nazarenes Believe About the Future Life?

We believe in the resurrection of the dead, that the bodies both of the just and of the unjust shall be raised to life and united with their spirits—"they that have done good, unto the resurrection of life; and they that have done evil, unto the resurrection of damnation." . . . We believe that glorious and everlasting life is assured to all who savingly believe in, and obediently follow, Jesus Christ our Lord; and that the finally impenitent shall suffer eternally in hell.[9]

Either there is a heaven or there isn't; Nazarenes believe there is—and are sincerely trying to get there themselves and are earnestly trying to take as many with them as possible. Either there is a hell or there isn't; Nazarenes believe there is—and are doing their utmost to shun it and to turn as many as possible away from it.

What Is the Church of the Nazarene?

A brief but adequate answer to this question is given by Dr. J. B. Chapman, late general superintendent in the Church of the Nazarene, when he says:

The Church of the Nazarene is an orthodox Protestant church, holding to all the historic doctrines of the New Testament, but especially emphasizing the Wesleyan doctrine of sanctification or perfect love. This doctrine, in brief, holds that we must be made holy in heart while in this life, and that this state of holiness is not attained at the time of justification or regeneration, but that it is received by faith at some time subsequent to regeneration, is wrought by the Holy Spirit, and can be attained by the grace of God while we yet live in a world in which sin abounds.

This church is not a cult, but preaches to all men regardless of race or standing, and believes its message is adapted to all. Its members are those who have believed its doctrines, who have testified to having received definite Christian experience, and who have been publicly received into the fellowship of the church.[10]

It is important to remember that the Church of the Nazarene is not a cult. It is a sect, becoming a church. As William Warren Sweet says, "Several American religious bodies are now in the transitional stage from sect to church. The Church of the Nazarene furnishes an example."[11] And, as Dr. Sweet continues, "A basic difference between a sect and a cult is that the sect carries on within the Christian tradition, the cult largely outside that framework."[12]

No one, surely, can read the above doctrinal statements and doubt that the Church of the Nazarene is carrying on in the orthodox Christian tradition. And may it be said with deep gratitude to God that even in the peculiar and powerful pressures of a transitional phase the Church of the Nazarene is keeping true to its mission and its message of HOLINESS EVANGELISM, which alone called it into being and which alone justifies its existence.

Why, then, am I a Nazarene?

1. I am a Nazarene because of inheritance and because of personal choice.

2. I am a Nazarene because the Church of the Nazarene teaches and proclaims the deity of Jesus Christ—without equivocation and without apology.

3. I am a Nazarene because the Church of the Nazarene teaches that the Bible is the inspired Word of God and that it is a sufficient guide, for every man, for the difficult journey from earth to heaven.

4. I am a Nazarene because the Church of the Nazarene teaches and proclaims that salvation is not by works of man but by faith in the atoning blood of Jesus Christ.

5. I am a Nazarene because the Church of the Nazarene unblinkingly faces the fact that sin is the deepest problem in human life but proclaims that the saving and sanctifying grace of Christ is the only adequate answer.

6. I am a Nazarene because the Church of the Nazarene teaches that it is possible for a surrendered and obedient soul to be cleansed from all sin—and to know it, and to live that life of holiness through the indwelling power of the Holy Spirit.

7. I am a Nazarene because the Church of the Nazarene, through its disciplines and standards, challenges to that high level of ethics consistent with the concept of holiness.

8. I am a Nazarene because the Church of the Nazarene was not founded by a deceived and deceiving charlatan, but claims as it human founders dedicated and devoted men whose doctrine and dynamic of holiness found their source, not in Wesley or in Luther or in Calvin or in Augustine or in Isaiah or in Moses—but in the eternal and holy God, who said, "Be ye holy; for I am holy" (I Pet. 1:16); and in His Son, who said, "Be ye therefore perfect, even as your Father which is in heaven is perfect" (Matt. 5:48).

9. I am a Nazarene because the human leaders of the Church of the Nazarene are not only aggressive enough to challenge Nazarenes to give more, to witness more, and to win more, but are also spiritual enough to plead with Nazarenes to pray more and to cry more and to believe more, so that the redemptive mission of the church can be more effectively realized.

10. I am a Nazarene because in seventeen years of evangelism in the Church of the Nazarene, in over four hundred revivals across America and around the world, I have never been asked—by *anyone*—to dilute the message, to compromise the standards, or to alter the methods of holiness evangelism. And for this I say a glad and grateful "Praise God!"

We are not meant to remain as children at the mercy of every chance wind of teaching and the jockeying of men who are expert in the crafty presentation of lies. But we are meant to hold firmly to the truth in love, and to grow up in every way into Christ, the Head.

—Eph. 4:14-15 (Phillips)

Chapter Two

WHY I AM A NAZARENE

and Not a Mormon

WHAT IS A MORMON?

Strictly speaking, there is no such thing as a "Mormon," and there is no "Mormon" church. "Mormon" is merely a nickname for a member of the Church of Jesus Christ of Latter-day Saints.[1] Just as converts to the Church of Christ in the first century came to be called Christians, so in the nineteenth century those who professed belief in the *Book of Mormon* were called Mormons.[2] Mormons would prefer to be called Latter-day Saints. And that is understandable, considering the bizarre beginnings and contents of the *Book of Mormon,* whence they get their name.

WHAT IS THE "BOOK OF MORMON"?

It is a book which was first published in the year 1830 in the little town of Palmyra, New York. The book has fifteen divisions which are purportedly the records of prehistoric America, tracing the original inhabitants of America to various Jewish tribes and covering several thousand years from the time of the Tower of Babel to about A.D. 400.

The book, so Mormons believe, is a translation of "reformed Egyptian hieroglyphics" written on some gold plates which were found in 1826 by young Joseph Smith on the side of the hill Cumorah, near Palmyra, New York. Along with these gold plates were found some magic spectacles, "stones set in silver bows," which were called

Urim and Thummim. With the aid of these miraculous stones Joseph Smith was not only able to read the strange hieroglyphics on the plates, but was also able to translate the weird story, which translation was dictated by him, from behind a curtain, to a farmer, Martin Harris, and a country schoolteacher, Oliver Cowdery.

This is the book that Mormons not only accept as the most important source book for their beliefs and doctrines, but also accept as equally inspired with the Holy Bible.

WHAT IS THE STORY THE "BOOK OF MORMON" TELLS?

It tells first how Christ came to a certain Lehi in the time of King Zedekiah, and how Lehi's four sons, Laman, Lemuel, Nephi, and Sam, in order to escape persecution built a ship and left Jerusalem and landed on the southwestern coast of South America. A little later two of Lehi's sons, Nephi and Laman, had a falling out and began warring with one another. God was displeased with the Lamanites and cursed them with a dark skin, and they became the ancestors of the American Indian.

The Nephites, however, found favor with God and began to migrate northward and at about the time of Christ settled in Central America. There they found the descendants of another Jewish tribe, also emigrants in the time of Zedekiah, who preserved the records, written on gold plates, of still a third tribe, the mysterious Jaredites, who had crossed the Atlantic after the fall of the Tower of Babel but had recently been totally destroyed in a civil war.

Just after Christ's resurrection, according to the *Book of Mormon,* Christ came to America and established His Church among the Nephites. In about the year A.D. 385, however, the heathen Lamanites were so completely destroying the Christian Nephites that Mormon, the great military leader and prophet and priest of the Nephites, gathered up all the records of his predecessors and wrote their abbreviated history on some gold plates, which he gave to his son, Moroni.

In a tremendous battle near the hill Cumorah, in western New York, Mormon and all the Nephites were destroyed—only Moroni was spared. When Moroni had completed the records he buried them in the hill Cumorah, where fifteen hundred years later he appeared as an angel to a country boy by the name of Joseph Smith, who found the golden plates exactly where the angel Moroni had directed him.

And the translation of those golden plates, discovered and translated by Joseph Smith, is the story the *Book of Mormon* tells—a story actually believed by Mormons around the world.

What Does Research Reveal About the "Book of Mormon"?

In the early years of the nineteenth century, a Presbyterian minister by the name of Solomon Spaulding wrote a historic novel about the early inhabitants of the American continents. He called his novel "Manuscript Found." He took his novel to a printer in Pittsburgh, Pennsylvania, by the name of Patterson, but Mr. Patterson didn't think enough of it to print it. Mr. Spaulding left the manuscript in Patterson's print shop, however, and moved on to Ohio, where two years later, in 1816, at Conneaut, Ohio, he died of consumption.

The Mormons, of course, have tried to destroy such damaging evidence of fraud by publishing what they said was the genuine "Manuscript Story," which has no traces of the contents of the *Book of Mormon*. But this is not the "Manuscript Found" of Solomon Spaulding, as there are sworn affidavits of Spaulding's brother and others to the effect that "Manuscript Found" and the *Book of*

Mormon are one and the same so far as their historical parts are concerned.

Sidney Rigdon, a onetime Baptist preacher who had left the Baptist church and joined the Disciples, only to become embittered against the Disciples' leader, Alexander Campbell, often visited Patterson's print shop in Pittsburgh. There he found Spaulding's manuscript, was fascinated by it, and thought he saw in it a chance, with the addition of passages of scripture, to use it as a religious document to gain followers. Young Joseph Smith, who was already known for his use of "peep-stones" in searching for buried treasure, was the ideal accomplice in such a hoax.

The *Book of Mormon,* as Dr. Bates points out, "contains a number of chapters lifted bodily from the Old and New Testaments and is full of acknowledged quotations from them. Shakespeare was apparently known to Nephi, as he mentions 'the undiscovered country from whose bourne no traveller returns.' It is foretold that in due time a mighty prophet shall arise, 'by the name of Joseph,' who shall make known the contents of the records to future generations."[3]

Joseph Smith at first declared that no one but himself could see the plates and live. He later declared in the presence of sworn witnesses that his first-born would be allowed to open the plates. But his first-born was born dead. In March, 1829, he got a revelation that only three of that generation were to witness to the plates on the ground of having seen them. These three witnesses were Martin Harris, a farmer who put up the money to publish the book; David Whitmer, a friend at whose house the "translation" was made; and Oliver Cowdery, a country schoolteacher, who took Smith's dictation—from behind a curtain.

These three "witnesses" signed a statement, still published in the *Book of Mormon:* "We declare with words of soberness that an angel of God came down from heaven, and he brought and laid before our eyes, that we beheld and saw the plates, and the engravings thereon."

Harris later testified in court that he had seen the plates, "not as I do that pencil case," but "with the eye of faith . . . though at the time they were covered over with a cloth."

David Whitmer, in his eighty-second year, wrote a pamphlet in which he said that in 1849 the Lord had seen fit to manifest unto Cowdery and him the errors of doctrine into which the heads of the church had led them.

All three "witnesses" were later expelled from the Mormon church as thieves and liars, with Harris being called a "liar and swindler" by Joseph Smith himself, and Cowdery and Whitmer being chased out of Missouri by a crowd of Mormons, eighty of whom signed a statement that the two were thieves and counterfeiters.

Three of the second group of eight "witnesses" who had testified that they had "seen and hefted" the plates later repudiated Mormonism, and of the remaining five, three belonged to the Smith family. Even Joseph Smith's own first wife, Emma Hale Smith, left the church and denied that she had ever "credited her husband's visions or revelations," and two years after his death married L. C. Bidamon, a Nauvoo, Illinois, tavern keeper.[4]

Professor Charles Anthon, a renowned Egyptologist of New York City, to whom Martin Harris showed a copy of some of the hieroglyphics on the "plates," said in a letter to E. D. Howe, under the date of February 17, 1834: "The whole story about my pronouncing the Mormon inscription to be reformed Egyptian hieroglyphics is perfectly false. I soon came to the conclusion that it was all a trick—perhaps a hoax. The paper contained anything else but Egyptian hieroglyphics."[5]

It is indeed unfortnate that when Joseph Smith had finished the task of "translating," the angel Moroni took the gold plates and the magic glasses back to heaven. Those gold plates, six inches thick and fastened with "rings of gold," and those mysterious stones, would be of considerable interest today—to Mormons and to non-Mormons alike. But Moroni apparently felt that they could be entrusted only to young Joseph Smith, and even to him for a period of only a few months.

Horton Davies has a pertinent word when he says: "Our mystification at the linguistic expertness of this illiterate man is increased by the assurance of Egyptologists that Egyptian hieroglyphics remained unchanged from the fifth century B.C. until the fourth century A.D. Furthermore, not only is 'reformed Egyptian' unknown to the Egyptologists, but these experts themselves were unable to decipher Egyptian inscriptions until the discovery of the Rosetta stone. We are left to judge between a gigantic fraud and a great miracle, as the explanation of these events."[6]

This, then, is the book that is accepted as scripture, along with the Bible, by hundreds of thousands of sincere Americans called "Mormons," who believe that if the book is not true, then the entire structure of Mormonism is built on a false foundation.

Who Was Joseph Smith?

Joseph Smith was born in Sharon, Vermont, December 23, 1805. His parents were shiftless, illiterate "frontier-drifters," moving nineteen times in ten years from one unsuccessful farm to another, finally locating two miles from Manchester, in western New York.

Young Joseph's education and discipline were sadly neglected. He was considered by his more respectable neighbors as lazy, fond of lying, and, like his father, Joseph Smith, Sr., the victim of a habit of hunting for buried treasure by the aid of "peep-stones"—stones which he would place in his hat, which would then be pulled down over his eyes.

Young Joseph was also much addicted to visions. In fact, one of his first versions of the "plates" was that he had seen them in a dream and that they were guarded by a "man who appeared like a Spaniard, having a long beard down over his breast, with his throat cut from ear to ear and the blood streaming down."

It is quite understandable that a young man reared in an atmosphere of ignorance and superstition, and himself credulous and irresponsible, with blurred distinctions between fact and fantasy, should very early begin to receive visions and revelations.

These visions and revelations of a religious nature began when Joseph was fifteen years old, when the Lord appeared and told him that all the denominational churches were "wrong." Then at eighteen he was "called" to become a "prophet of the most High God," and soon after that the angel "Moroni" appeared to him and spoke to him about the mysterious "plates." Joseph Smith continued to receive visions and revelations until his death—at the hands of a mob, in 1844.

In two of the sacred volumes of the Mormons, the *Book of Commandments* (1833) and the *Doctrines and Covenants* (1835), are found no less than 124 revelations from the prophet Joseph Smith. In one of them the Lord announced to His prophet that the *Book of Mormon* must not be sold for less than $1.25 "on pain of death," except that Joseph Smith, Sr., might sell it at a lower price.

These revelations seemed to have come to Prophet Smith at exceedingly appropriate times. On the very day the Mormon church was organized, in Peter Whitmer's house at Fayette, New York, April 6, 1830, twenty-four-year-old Joseph Smith, who had just baptized Oliver Cowdery and had been baptized by him, received a revelation from the Lord that he was to be the leader and prophet of the new church of six members. Cowdery, however, did not indulge Joseph all his whims, and so the prophet received a very special revelation that Cowdery was to head west and preach to the "Lamanites."

All the twists and turnings of this strange "prophet" were covered over and explained by the magic word "revelation." His moving to Kirtland, Ohio, his building of several temples, his notorious banking venture, his outlawing of polygamy—and his subsequent reversal, his own plural marriages, his candidacy for the presidency of the United States, his moving to Missouri and then his escape to Illinois, his plan of tithing and missionary work for the "saints," his destruction of the printing press that was bringing charges against him, his going to the Carthage, Illinois, jail, where he was killed June 27, 1844— all the incredible eccentricities of an untrained mind filled with fantasy and with delusions of destiny—all found ready and immediate explanation to himself, and to his followers, by the one word "revelation."

This, then, is the man of whom one historian said, "If there is one fact in American history that can be regarded as definitely established it is that the engaging Joe Smith was a deliberate charlatan."[7] But it is also the same man of whom Richard L. Evans, a Mormon historian and a member of the Council of Twelve, could say: "Mormons look upon Joseph Smith as one who was commissioned of God to effect a 'restoration' of the Gospel of Jesus Christ and to open a new Gospel 'dispensation.' They look upon him as a prophet of God, in the same literal sense as they look upon other prophets of the Old and New Testaments."[8]

WHAT DO MORMONS MEAN BY "CELESTIAL MARRIAGE"?

Mormons distinguish between "temporal" and "celestial" marriage. Temporal marriage lasts only until death but "celestial" marriage is binding beyond death—it is eternal. To Mormons, the celestial marriage is of far greater importance than the marriage for time. For, so Mormons believe, celestial marriage is an eternal relationship between the sexes wherein a man retains his earthly wife, or wives, and begets children in heaven for all eternity.

As Joseph Fielding Smith, one of the Twelve Apostles of the Mormon church, says:

> Marriage is the grandest, most glorious and most exalted principle connected with the Gospel. It is that which the Lord holds in reserve for those who become his sons and daughters; all others are servants only, even if they gain salvation. They do not become members of the household of our Father and our God if they refuse to receive the celestial covenant of marriage.[9]

These celestial marriages can be contracted only by special rites in the Mormon temples, by parties who are deemed worthy and desirous of it. The Mormon church, however, solemnizes marriages outside of the temples in case the contracting parties are unworthy of the temple rite or are not desirous of it. While the husband and wife who are united in the temple are said to be "sealed," those united outside of the temple are only "married." When the couple is married outside of the temple the tie is binding only for time; it is dissolved at death. The contracting parties will no longer be husband and wife in eternity and hence will bear no children there. Such can never become "gods." But those who are "sealed" in marriage, so the Mormons believe, can look forward to having children in heaven and can ultimately attain the status of "gods."

Do Mormons Believe in Polygamy?

One of the most controversial tenets of the Mormon faith is that of polygamy. It is stoutly and hotly denied by the Mormons that plural marriages are contracted by the faithful today, even though occasionally national interest is focused on "splinter" groups of Mormons who are still found practicing it.

But on July 12, 1843, at Nauvoo, Illinois, Joseph Smith, the prophet, claimed to have received a revelation commanding polygamy and those who did not receive it were to be damned. In this revelation his wife, Emma Hale Smith, was commanded to receive all those who had been given unto her husband, Joseph Smith, and to cleave unto him and none else or be damned, and to forgive her husband, Joseph Smith, wherein he had already trespassed.

The Mormon theory that there are millions of pure spirits just waiting for bodies makes the belief in plural marriages almost a necessity.

"It is problematical," as one historian has said, "whether polygamy was introduced that men might obey the 'Gospel' and provide as many bodies as possible for the pre-existent souls or whether the theory of the pre-existence of souls was set up to justify the practice of polygamy."[10]

Criticism of the vicious and unchristian practice of polygamy became so intense and so widespread in America that Congress, in the late eighties, passed laws prohibiting the practice. But it was not until the Supreme Court upheld the law banning polygamy and declared the law constitutional that the Mormon church officially outlawed polygamy. It is significant to note, however, that the president of the Mormon church, Wilford Woodruff, banned polygamy in the church October 6, 1890, not because he considered it wrong, but because he deemed it expedient.

One must conclude, then, that Mormons, to be true to their stated beliefs as published in their official books, still believe in polygamy but do not practice it only because they are restrained and forbidden to do so by the civil laws of the land.

WHAT DO MORMONS MEAN BY "BAPTISM FOR THE DEAD"?

Mormons believe that preachers who have died are now preaching the gospel to the dead, and since the dead may believe and repent, but cannot be baptized, and since baptism is necessary to salvation, this rite may be undertaken for them by a living Mormon. It is a vicarious baptism for a departed loved one or friend who might otherwise miss the joys of heaven. This baptism, like the special rites of celestial marriage, is always performed in a Mormon temple.

It is impossible, of course, for a living proxy to know whether his work for the dead is efficacious. That depends entirely on whether the dead for whom he is baptized accepts or rejects the work done in his behalf. As Joseph Fielding Smith said:

> It has been decreed that man must do for himself what he is able to do; but what he cannot do for himself others may do for him. That is why Jesus Christ became our Redeemer. In a less capacity we may be saviors to others by doing for them in the temples what they cannot do for themselves and what we can do for them.[11]

I. WHAT DO MORMONS BELIEVE ABOUT CHRIST?

In answering this question for a popular magazine, Richard L. Evans, a noted Mormon and a member of the powerful Council of Twelve, said, "They [the Mormons] believe Him to be the Son of God. They believe in His atoning sacrifice and literal resurrection. They accept Him as the Savior and Redeemer of mankind."[12]

Now that sounds evangelical enough—if one does not read their doctrinal statements in their official publications. The distortion begins to show up, however, when one reads in Brigham Young's discourses, which are respected and believed by all true Mormons, such statements as the following:

When the Virgin Mary conceived the child Jesus, the Father had begotten Him in His own likeness. He was not begotten by the Holy Ghost. And who is the Father? He is the first of the human family. Jesus, our Elder Brother, was begotten in the flesh by the same character that was in the Garden of Eden, and who is our Father in heaven.[13]

How natural for Mormons to believe this when according to their own theologians God and Christ are only enlarged men! As Brigham Young said, "Our God and Father in heaven has a body, with parts, the same as you and I have." And Talmage, in *Articles of Faith,* said, "We know that both the Father and Son are in form and stature perfect men; each of them possesses a tangible body, infinitely pure and perfect and attended by transcendent glory, nevertheless, a body of flesh and bones."[14]

In other words, the real Mormon teaching concerning Christ is that Jesus is the son of Adam-God and Mary —not conceived by the Holy Ghost. It would be difficult to imagine a more symbolic heresy.

II. WHAT DO MORMONS BELIEVE ABOUT THE BIBLE?

Joseph Smith, the prophet, says in the Articles of Faith, number 8: "We believe the Bible to be the word of God as far as it is translated correctly; we also believe the *Book of Mormon* to be the word of God."[15]

That phrase, "as far as it is translated correctly," is a treacherous one, as it opens the way for all manner of wresting and twisting of scripture to sanction the beliefs and actions of men of bigoted minds and perverted morals.

The Mormon theory of progressive revelations actually destroys the finality and uniqueness of God's Word as expressed in the Bible. Mormons deny the finality of the Bible when they say, "The canon scripture is not only *not* final, but the Lord has greater things to reveal to the people than have yet been given."[16]

This theory of modern revelation is fundamental in Mormon theology. The official statement of doctrine is:

> We believe all that God has revealed, all that he does now reveal, and we believe that he will yet reveal many great and important things pertaining to the Kingdom of God.[17]

A noted Mormon authority wrote recently that, while the Bible is the Word of God, the Mormons recognize that errors have crept into it, and so it is not a fully dependable and complete guide. And because of this, the Latter-day Saints have three other books which "supplement" the Bible, these three being the *Book of Mormon,* the *Doctrine and Covenants,* and the *Pearl of Great Price.*[18]

But it is in the "supplements" to the Bible that the distortions slip in and heresies are born.

III. WHAT DO MORMONS BELIEVE ABOUT SALVATION?

For one thing, the Mormon believes that one must believe in Joseph Smith and the *Book of Mormon* to be saved.

While the words repentance and faith are pronounced by the Mormon, and much is made of baptism, which is "for forgiveness of sins," the Mormon believes that the atonement of Christ covered original sin only —a universal release from the "mortal death" incident to the sin of Adam—and a means of propitiation for individual sin, which salvation may be "attained" by subsequent obedience and good works of the sinner.

Mormons believe, in effect, in ultimate universal salvation. Only the "sons of perdition" will be finally lost. Only those, however, who have been obedient to "all the ordinances and commandments of the Kingdom" will be "exalted," that is, have the privilege of eventually becoming gods, where they will "create worlds and populate them" with the offspring of their "celestial wives."

The emphasis throughout is not upon faith in the finished work of Jesus Christ, but rather upon "attaining" salvation through obedience to ordinances and rules —the rules and ordinances, of course, of the Mormon church.

IV. What Do Mormons Believe About the Future Life?

Mormons accept fully the idea of the immortality of man.

> Energy, matter, and intelligence exist externally and are indestructible. And man himself has existed from the premortal past and will continue with his individual identity, into the endless eternal future.[19]

In the life to come, according to a contemporary Mormon writer, men will not be arbitrarily divided into two fixed groups—inhabitants of heaven and hell. Jesus stated, "In my Father's house are *many* mansions." There will be various levels of existence. Individuality will be retained. Life is purposeful. It is progressive. It leads to godhood.[20]

Or, as Evans says:

> The heaven the Mormon looks to and lives for is a real place of eternal progress, with endless association with loved ones, with families and friends. For those who are willfully indifferent to their opportunities on earth, the knowledge that they have fallen short of their highest possible happiness will be part of the punishment of the "hell" of the hereafter.[21]

Mormons believe that for those who have failed to fulfill the conditions of salvation in this life there is still a chance beyond the grave. There will be punishment both here and in a future life, but it will not be everlasting. Only the "sons of perdition" will be finally and utterly lost and damned. But one of the greatest

Mormon leaders asserted that "these were so few that they could be counted on the fingers of one hand."[22]

Mormons believe that at the moment of death the righteous—those who have obeyed the laws and ordinances of the Mormon church, and submitted to its priesthood—will be ushered into a state of happiness—paradise—to await the resurrection. The evil go away into darkness.[23]

After death and during the millennium, Mormons believe, those who did not obey the ordinances of the gospel while here on earth will be preached to and will have a chance to repent and believe—and through the Mormon practice of vicarious baptism by living Mormons for their dead, those who died in their sins will be saved and will be in heaven, where they will be, in effect, second-class citizens to those who have been "exalted" and on their way to becoming "gods."

As Joseph Fielding Smith said of the wicked during the millennium:

> Their punishment will be for their good. Their suffering must be met, for they have decried the mercies of Jesus Christ and therefore must suffer even as he suffered for the sins of the world, for his suffering will not cleanse them. It will be a punishment of cleansing; and when they have paid the price—then shall they be prepared to receive such blessings as the Lord, in his great mercy, is prepared to give them.[24]

To those who die in the "faith"—have been obedient to all the laws and ordinances of the Mormon church—the promise of eventual godhood is proclaimed:

> Shall we not continue on to perfection after the resurrection? Latter-day Saints believe in this progression in eternity until, eventually, we become worthy through knowledge, wisdom, humility, and obedience, to be like God, and then to have the privilege of being made equal in power, might and dominion.[25]

WITH SUCH BELIEFS, CAN THE MORMONS BE RESPECTED?

Indeed so. In spite of their distorted doctrines many of the Mormons, as persons, are intelligent, sincere, ethical, good neighbors, and exemplary citizens. The state of Utah, which is 70 per cent Mormon, has a nationwide—even world-wide—reputation for its excellence in the fields of public education, health, and social services.

Clean in their personal habits—they do not use alcohol or tobacco or other "deleterious" substances which impair health and well-being.

Faithful in their giving—tithing is an article of their religion.

Zealous in missionary activity—more than 4,000 young Mormons go out two by two each year as missionaries without compensation, giving a year or more to the work of spreading the teaching of their church at home and abroad.[26]

With the most tempestuous history of any church body in the United States, they have grown until the Church of Jesus Christ of Latter-day Saints, with headquarters in Salt Lake City, Utah, has 1,246,352 members in 3,300 congregations around the world.[27]

Why, then, am I a Nazarene and not a Mormon?

1. I am not a Mormon because, as a Nazarene, I believe that God is a Spirit—

God is a Spirit: and they that worship him must worship him in spirit and in truth (John 4:24),

and so I could never believe in the Mormon God, who has "flesh and bones," and who will ultimately share His creatorship and omnipotent power and dominion with mere men who have risen to "godhood."

2. I am not a Mormon because, as a Nazarene, I believe that Christ is God's Son in an eternal uniqueness—

In the beginning was the Word, and the Word was with God, and the Word was God. The same was in the beginning with God. All things were made by him; and without him was not any thing made that was made (John 1:1-3),

and so I could never believe in the Mormon Christ, who is merely the son of Adam-God and Mary.

3. I am not a Mormon because, as a Nazarene, I believe that the Bible is the inspired Word of God and that in the Bible is the complete revelation of God's demands for salvation—

But these are written, that ye might believe that Jesus is the Christ, the Son of God; and that believing ye might have life through his name (John 20:31),

and so I could never believe in the Mormon "Bibles"— the *Book of Mormon*, etc., which are of human origin and are nothing but fanciful stories, incredible history, distorted geography, and the "cunningly devised fables" of warped and twisted minds.

4. I am not a Mormon because, as a Nazarene, I believe that salvation is wholly by grace on God's part—

Being justified freely by his grace through the redemption that is in Christ Jesus (Rom. 3:24);

and by faith on man's part—

For by grace are ye saved through faith; and that not of yourselves: it is the gift of God: not of works, lest any man should boast (Eph. 2:8-9),

and so I could never believe in the Mormon salvation by obedience to the ordinances and commandments of the Mormon church as ruled by its "priesthood."

5. I am not a Mormon because, as a Nazarene, I believe in a future life of rewards and punishments—

These shall go away into everlasting punishment: but the righteous into life eternal (Matt. 25:46), and so I could never believe in the Mormon heaven of first- and second-class citizens, where the "exalted" would finally become "gods" in their own right, and in the Mormon hell, where "less than the number of fingers on one hand" would suffer punishment for their sins.

6. I am not a Mormon because, as a Nazarene, I believe that Christ will personally appear and those who are ready will rise to meet Him in the air—

For the Lord himself shall descend from heaven with a shout, with the voice of the archangel, and with the trump of God: and the dead in Christ shall rise first: then we which are alive and remain shall be caught up together with them in the clouds, to meet the Lord in the air: and so shall we ever be with the Lord (I Thess. 4:16-17),

and so I could never believe in the Mormon millennium, where those who have died in their sins will have another chance to make the right choice.

It is appointed unto men once to die, but after this the judgment (Heb. 9:27).

7. I am not a Mormon because, as a Nazarene, I believe that at the moment of death one's destiny is forever sealed—

And I saw the dead, small and great, stand before God; and the books were opened: and another book was opened, which is the book of life: and the dead were judged out of those things which were written in the books, according to their works (Rev. 20:12),

and so I could never believe in the Mormon theory of baptism for the dead, whereby a living proxy could take the place of a dead sinner.

8. I am not a Mormon because, as a Nazarene, I believe that in heaven there will be neither marriage nor giving in marriage—

For in the resurrection they neither marry, nor are given in marriage, but are as the angels of God in heaven (Matt. 22:30),

and so I could never believe in the Mormon theory of "celestial" marriage, where men and women will continue to have children through eternity.

9. I am not a Mormon because, as a Nazarene, I believe that one man should be married to only one living woman—

Let every man have his own wife, and let every woman have her own husband (I Cor. 7:2),

and so I could never believe the vicious, if expediently banned, Mormon doctrine of polygamy.

10. I am not a Mormon because, as a Nazarene, I believe that a true prophet must be holy—

For the prophecy came not in old time by the will of man: but holy men of God spake as they were moved by the Holy Ghost (II Pet. 1:21),

and so I could never believe the ridiculous theories about the credulous and dictatorial and sensual Joseph Smith being a prophet of God, or that he was "inspired" when he wrote the *Book of Mormon* and other works called "sacred" by Mormons.

In those days there were false prophets, just as there will be false teachers among you today. They will be men who will subtly introduce dangerous heresies. They will thereby deny the Lord who redeemed them, and it will not be long before they bring on themselves their own downfall. Many will follow their pernicious teaching and thereby bring discredit on the way of truth.

—II Pet. 2:1-2 (Phillips)

Chapter Three

WHY I AM A NAZARENE

and Not a Roman Catholic

WHAT IS A ROMAN CATHOLIC?

Every born-again Christian is a "catholic"—that is, a member of the universal society of saved souls. But a Roman Catholic is one who has been baptized by the Roman Catholic church and subscribes unquestioningly to its traditions and dogmas and is governed, in all religious and moral matters, by the totalitarian authority of the heirarchy headed by the "infallible" pope in Rome.

WHAT DO ROMAN CATHOLICS BELIEVE ABOUT THEIR CHURCH?

They believe that the Roman Catholic church is the only true church, and that all who willfully reject her claims will be damned. Roman Catholics deny that their church is just another religious denomination of Christendom; they believe that the Roman Catholic church is THE church, and that all other churches are spurious and will ultimately go down in defeat.

Here is the oath, for instance, that each convert to the Roman Catholic church must take:

> I (name), having before my eyes the Holy Gospels, which I touch with my hand, and knowing that no one can be saved without that faith which the Holy, Catholic, Apostolic, Roman Church holds, believes and teaches: against which I grieve that I have greatly erred, inasmuch as I have held and believed doctrines opposed to her teaching;

I now, by the help of God's grace, profess that I believe the Holy, Catholic, Apostolic, Roman Church, to be the only true Church established on earth by Jesus Christ to which I submit myself with my whole heart. I firmly believe all the articles which she proposes to my belief, and I reject and condemn all that she rejects and condemns, and I am ready to observe all that she commands me.[1]

What Do Roman Catholics Believe About the Pope?

Roman Catholics believe the pope to be the "head of the Church," the "vicar of Christ," and when he speaks "ex cathedra," or intentionally and officially on matters of faith and morals, that he is infallible.

It has taken centuries, however, for the "Bishop of Rome" to rise to the place of supremacy which he occupies today. As late as the fifth century the supervision of all of Christendom was shared by five city bishops, or patriarchs: those of Rome, Constantinople, Antioch, Alexandria, and Jerusalem. The Bishop of Rome had special prestige because he was in the Imperial City, the capital of the Roman Empire.

In the seventh century the Saracens conquered Antioch, Jerusalem, and Alexandria, destroying the churches of those cities and their power, leaving only Constantinople as a rival to Rome. In 1054 the "Great Schism" came between Rome and Constantinople and the Bishop of Rome, as head of the Western Church, assumed more and more power until during the time of Pope Gregory VII (A.D. 1073-85) the Bishop of Rome usurped the exclusive use of the title "Pope." Before that time all bishops were called popes and in the Eastern branch of the Church even the priests were called "popes."[2]

The peculiar prestige and incredible power of the Roman pope stems from the Roman Catholic belief that he is a lineal successor to the Apostle Peter, who was supposed to have founded the church at Rome. All Roman Catholics believe that Peter, in the last years of his life, went to Rome, where he became bishop and

began to exercise the power that Christ conferred upon
him when He said, "Upon this rock I will build my
church," etc. Roman Catholics believe that those powers
were passed on to the successive Roman bishops and that
they in turn receive from God authority over all Christians.

As the power and prestige of the papacy increased,
additional authority was assumed by the individual popes,
until in the year 1870 the dogma of the infallibility of the
pope was proclaimed, but it was only a proclamation of a
belief that had been almost universally held by all faithful Catholics for several hundred years. The Council
of Trent, for instance, in the sixteenth century, announced:

> We define that the Holy Apostolic See and the Roman
> Pontiff holds the primacy over the whole world, and the
> Roman Pontiff himself is the successor of the Blessed
> Peter, prince of the Apostles, and the true Vicar of
> Christ, the head of the whole church, the father of all
> Christians; and that to him, in the person of Blessed Peter,
> was given, by Our Lord Jesus Christ, full power to feed,
> rule, and govern the universal church, as is contained
> also in the acts of the ecumenical councils, and in the
> sacred canons.

This power of the papacy, assumed and usurped,
became so absolute that Pope Pius X could announce:

> The Pope is not only the representative of Jesus Christ,
> but He is Jesus Christ Himself, hidden under the veil of
> the flesh. Does the Pope speak? It is Jesus Christ that
> speaks. Does the Pope accord a favor or pronounce an
> anathema? It is Jesus Christ who pronounces the anathema
> or accords the favor.

In the nineteen hundred years since Christ there
have been 261 "successors" to Peter, some of them im-
moral, corrupt, and profligate men; and yet each one
of these men, so Roman Catholics believe, received his
power and authority directly from Christ's statement to
Peter—and the perversion of the meaning of that state-

ment has been the fount from which have flowed the poisons and corruptions and twisted doctrines that have enslaved generations of men in terrifying bonds of fear and superstition and ignorance.

There is not a shred of evidence that Jesus, or the apostles, or the Early Church, gave to Peter any primacy or sole authority. To the end of Jesus' life, the apostles disputed as to who was the greatest among them, and there is no record that Jesus gave final authority to Peter. St. Paul's position among the gentile Christians was certainly as high as St. Peter's among the Jewish, and in all of Paul's controversies, even with Jewish Christians, he never appealed to St. Peter's authority, but insisted upon his own, even withstanding Peter "to his face." Christ, and Christ alone, is the only One who is referred to in the New Testament as the Head of the Church, and He is the only One in the entire New Testament called the Chief Shepherd.

What a picture in contrasts is the Christ of the seamless robe, rejected and despised of men, with no place to lay His head and no place to call His home, who moved and taught among the lowly and despised and had nothing but scorn and contempt for the priests and "popes" of His day—how strange the contrast between Him and His so-called "vicar," the pope, who is carried, not on a donkey, but on the shoulders of men—a "shepherd" carried by his "sheep"—who rules in splendid isolation his own little Vatican City, and claims absolute religious authority over almost thirty-five million Roman Catholics in the United States, and almost four hundred million around the world!

WHAT DO ROMAN CATHOLICS BELIEVE ABOUT MARY?

They believe that Mary was immaculately conceived, which is not to be confused with the belief in the Virgin Birth. All evangelical Christians believe in the virgin birth of Christ, but Roman Catholics believe also in the immaculate conception of Mary.

The dogma of the Immaculate Conception is the Roman Catholic belief that the Virgin Mary alone, of all human persons, since she would be the vehicle for the divine incarnation, was exempt from original sin from the moment she was conceived in the womb of her mother, St. Anne, and that she possessed fullness of grace; that never for an instant of her life was she without sanctifying grace and so never for a moment was she tainted with original sin.

This dogma of the Immaculate Conception, which all Roman Catholics must believe, was not defined as dogma until December 8, 1854. But again, the announcement of this dogma, like that of the infallibility of the pope, was only a formal announcement of a belief that had been accepted for many years, even though some of the greatest and earliest theologians of the Roman church, such as Augustine and St. Thomas Aquinas, along with a half dozen earlier popes, had opposed the teaching. In fact, the universal testimony of the Roman church for over ten centuries was that Mary was not immaculately conceived. Thomas Aquinas called the whole idea a "superstition." Nevertheless, in 1854, an "infallible" Roman pope decreed that to be a Christian one must believe in the Immaculate Conception—that Mary was free from original sin even from the moment of her conception.

Roman Catholics not only believe that Mary was born without original sin; they believe her to be the "Mediatrix" of all graces. Some even assert that no grace is given to anyone unless it first passes through Mary's hands. And this has led millions of Roman Catholics, in actual practice, to replace Christ with Mary, until a whole "cult of Mary" has arisen within the church

—and with the sanction, and even encouragement, of the hierarchy.

This "encouragement" has increased until today there are those of the hierarchy who are predicting that by the year 2000 it will be announced and defined as dogma that "the Blessed Virgin Mary is Co-Redemptrix of the human race." Even now, as James Nicholas reminds us, "The sanction of Rome supports the affirmations of the theologians who deny that any man can be saved without the protection of the Virgin, and assert that even God obeys her 'command.' "[3]

One of the most famous American cardinals, James Cardinal Gibbons, wrote:

> Never will our prayers find readier acceptance than when offered through her [Mary] . . . . She would be the instrument of God in feeding us with Divine grace, in clothing us with the garments of innocence, in sheltering us from the storms of temptations, in wiping away the stains of sin from our soul.[4]

And in *Our Lady of the Rosary,* a pamphlet issued in 1944 with the imprimatur of Archbishop (now Cardinal) Spellman of New York are found these words of petition to Mary:

> Sweet Heart of Jesus, be my love.
> Sweet Heart of Mary, be my salvation.
> O Mary Immaculate, great Mediatrix of all men . . .
> O Mary Immaculate, Refuge of Sinners, to whom will we go
>   if not to you?[5]

Is it any wonder, then, that Roman Catholics, with such ecclesiastical sanction and encouragement, not only venerate the statues and relics of Mary, but actually *pray* to her to intercede with her Son—as though Mary, or any other human, could be more merciful than Jesus Christ himself!

And yet that is the deepening belief of Roman Catholics everywhere. As Liguori, whose writings at the time of his canonization were declared to be absolutely free from error, wrote:

> He who is under the protection of Mary will be saved; he who is not will be lost. . . . O Immaculate Virgin, we are under thy protection, and therefore we have recourse to thee alone, and we beseech thee to prevent thy beloved Son, who is irritated by our sins, from abandoning us to the power of the devil. . . . Thou [Mary] art my only hope. . . . Lady in heaven, we have but one advocate, and that is thyself, and thou alone art truly loving and solicitous for our salvation. . . . My Queen and my Advocate with thy Son, whom I dare not approach.[6]

What a Christ-dishonoring belief—this subtle, satanic substitution of Mary for Christ! What a distortion of the words of Jesus Christ himself, who said: "And whatsoever ye shall ask in my name, that will I do, that the Father may be glorified in the Son. If ye shall ask any thing in my name, I will do it" (John 14: 13-14)! What an outright denial of the love and tender mercy of the Christ of whom John wrote: "We have an advocate with the Father, Jesus Christ the righteous" (I John 2: 1)!

As though the doctrine of the Immaculate Conception and the belief in Mary as the mediatrix of all the graces were not enough strain on credulity, the dogma of the Assumption of the Blessed Virgin Mary has now been proclaimed by the pope, and every Roman Catholic in the world must believe it. This is the belief that Mary's body, without undergoing the corruption of the grave, was reunited to her soul, and that in this state Mary was taken into heaven.

Even though this belief in the Assumption of Mary was generally accepted by Roman Catholics from the seventh century on, it was not defined as dogma by the pope until November of 1950. Since that time, however, it has been mandatory for every Roman Catholic to believe it.

Not one of these distorted beliefs about Mary can be substantiated by the Bible. They are rather, and significantly enough, mere figments of the fertile imaginations of celibate priests and popes.

One can thus see the development of the "cult of Mary" from its earliest beginnings to the announcement, in 1054, of the Immaculate Conception; to the announcement, in 1950, of the Assumption of the Blessed Virgin; to the belief in Mary as coredemptrix of the human race, which in all practical ways is already accepted as fact and awaits only the official pronouncement by the "infallible" pope in Rome for it to become mandatory upon all Roman Catholics for salvation.

WHAT IS THE ROSARY?

Strictly speaking, the Rosary is a prayer. Beads are used, however, in counting the prayers, and so the Rosary beads are sometimes confused with the Rosary itself. The prayer itself is composed of the Lord's Prayer, the "Glory Be to the Father," and a portion of the annunciation to Mary of the coming birth of Jesus, or the "Hail Mary," which is as follows: "Hail Mary, full of grace! The Lord is with thee: blessed art thou amongst women, and blessed is the fruit of thy womb, Jesus. Holy Mary, Mother of God, pray for us sinners, now and at the hour of our death. Amen."[7]

In praying the Rosary, a Roman Catholic makes the sign of the cross and then repeats the Apostles' Creed, then repeats the Lord's Prayer, then three "Hail Mary's," then a "Glory Be to the Father," and another "Our Father," then ten "Hail Mary's." One "Our Father," one "Glory Be to the Father," and ten "Hail Mary's," are known as a *decade* of the Rosary, and this last sequence is repeated fifteen times. During these prayers, the worshiper is supposed to meditate on fifteen different events in the life of Christ and Mary.

WHAT DO ROMAN CATHOLICS BELIEVE ABOUT THE MASS?

Every Roman Catholic believes the words of the Council of Trent which said:

> 1. There is in the Roman Catholic Church a true sacrifice, the mass, instituted by Jesus Christ; it is the sacrifice of the body and blood of Christ under the appearances of bread and wine.

> 2. This sacrifice is identical with the sacrifice of the Cross, inasmuch as Jesus Christ is priest and victim both. The only difference lies in the manner of offering, which is bloody upon the cross and bloodless on our altars.

> 3. It is a propitiatory sacrifice, atoning for our sins, and the sins of the living and of the dead in Christ, for whom it is offered.[3]

If there is any doubt in a Roman Catholic mind about the importance of the Mass, Pope Pius IV clarified it when he said, "If any man shall say that in the Mass there is not offered to God a true and proper sacrifice, let him be accursed."

The priest, in the sacrifice of the Mass, takes unleavened bread and grape wine to the altar. Then he kisses the "sepulchre," the cavity in every altar stone which must contain the relics (pieces of bone, clothing, hair, etc.) of at least two martyrs, and then, after an involved ceremony, the priest says in Latin, "This is my body," and as he says this, so a Roman Catholic believes, the bread ceases to be bread and becomes the body of Jesus Christ. As he says, "This is my blood," the wine ceases to be wine and becomes the blood of Jesus Christ. "The bread does not become the *symbol* cf Jesus' body, nor is His body present merely after a *spiritual* manner, nor is it present *along* with the bread. The substance *bread* ceases to be bread and becomes flesh. Likewise, the wine becomes the actual blood of Jesus. This is called 'transubstantiation'—the changing over of the substance. . . . In receiving Communion, Roman Catholic laymen are permitted to partake only of the 'Body' of Christ;

since the twelfth century the drinking of the 'Blood' has been reserved for the priest."[9]

Roman Catholics believe that every time the Mass is said (and one is said in Roman Catholic churches somewhere four times a second) the death of Christ on Calvary is repeated. "There on the altar Jesus Christ takes again upon himself the sins of men and again is offered up to appease the wrath of God angry with the wickedness of His children. There is but one difference, in Roman Catholic belief, between the sacrifice on the cross and the sacrifice on the altar: the one was bloody and the other is not."[10]

Rev. John O'Brien, one of the most popular Roman Catholic authors, writes:

> When the priest pronounces the tremendous words of consecration, he reaches up into the heavens, brings Christ down from His throne and places Him upon the altar to be offered up again as the Victim for the sins of man. It is a greater power than that of monarchs and potentates . . . , than that of saints and angels . . . , than that of Seraphim and Cherubim. Indeed, it is greater even than the power of the Virgin Mary. For, while the Blessed Virgin was the human agency by which Christ became incarnate a single time, the priest brings Christ down from the altar as the eternal Victim for the sins of man—not once but a thousand times! The priest speaks and lo! Christ, the eternal and omnipotent God, bows His head in humble obedience to the priest's command.[11]

Jesus did say, concerning the Last Supper, "This do in remembrance of me" (Luke 22:19). But there is no scripture to substantiate the Roman contention that a Roman Catholic priest has some strange and magic power to actually change bread into the flesh of Jesus and wine into the blood of Jesus.

There is no scripture exhorting Christians to celebrate the Mass. And not only is there not one word about this sacrifice in the New Testament; there is no account of the apostles or early Christians ever celebrating the Mass. And for Christians in any age to do so is to deny the scriptural teaching that "by one offering he hath perfected for ever them that are sanctified" (Heb. 10:14); and "who needeth not daily, as these high priests, to offer up sacrifice, first for his own sins, and then for the people's: for this he did once, when he offered up himself" (Heb. 7:27). Jesus Christ sent the apostles out to preach the gospel—He never once told them to "say" the Mass.

The whole system of the sacrifice of the Mass, as the Roman Catholic church practices it, is taken directly from pagan rituals and has been incorporated into the Roman tradition and raised to the level of high and colorful religious ceremony by the Roman Catholic church. But it is still pagan, and it is a pernicious perversion of the completed atonement of Jesus Christ.

I. WHAT DO ROMAN CATHOLICS BELIEVE ABOUT CHRIST?

To their everlasting credit, Roman Catholics definitely believe in the deity of Jesus Christ. To a Roman Catholic, Jesus was not just a good man in the forefront of all good men; He was and is the Son of God. There are some Protestants who accept the divinity of Jesus, but deny His deity. But a Roman Catholic believes that Christ is very God of very God; that Christ was God from all eternity, and Man from the time of His human birth.

To a Roman Catholic, and to every true Christian, Christ was more than man—He was God-Man—the Son of God in an eternally unique sense. Not that God became man, but that as God, He assumed human nature, so that in the one Person, Jesus Christ, there are the two natures, the divine and the human.

One can but admire the Roman Catholic's steadfast belief in the deity of Christ. And if it were not for its accretions of Bible-denying traditions and Christ-belittling

Mariolatry, the Roman Catholic church could have been the greatest redemptive agency in the history of the world. But its man-made traditions, its build-up of Mary, and its priest-ridden system so hide and overshadow and obstruct the view of the real Christ that millions who have traveled the road to Rome have tragically missed the way to Christ.

There are those Roman Catholics, however, who in their sincerity and hunger and faith have looked beyond the man-made traditions and above the robe-wrapped figure of a Virgin and right through the rigid rituals of the priests, until they have seen Jesus. And in humility and trust they have made Him Lord and Master of their lives, and instead of saying, "I am of Rome," or, "I am of Mary," they are able to say with glad and loving gratitude in their hearts, "I am of Christ."

II. What Do Roman Catholics Believe About the Bible?

Roman Catholics believe the Bible is a revelation from God to man, but that the Bible must be "interpreted" by the "infallible" Roman Catholic church before it can be rightly understood and before it is safe to read or to take as a guide for life. These "interpretations" along with the decrees of popes and councils are known as "traditions," and these traditions, to a Roman Catholic, are of equal authority with the Bible.

The continuing teaching of the Roman Catholic church is that the Bible is a dark Book, hard to understand, and is inadequate and insufficient and needs the supplementation which only the Roman Catholic church can provide. It is a fact of history that the Roman Catholic church, when possible, has prohibited the reading of the Bible, and when that was impossible, discouraged it. And even today, in predominantly Roman Catholic countries, the Bible is an unknown Book to the Roman Catholics. And in America, where the Roman Catholic church pretends to encourage its members to read the Bible, all that one needs to do is to quote or read to a Roman Catholic some familiar passage of scripture— known by almost any Protestant Sunday school pupil —to be convinced of the appalling ignorance and un-familiarity with the Bible of the average Roman Catholic.

The attitude of many Roman Catholics, both clergy and laity, toward the Bible is expressed in the words of Thomas F. Coakley: "The Catholic Church existed be-fore the Bible; it is possible for the Catholic Church to exist without the Bible, for the Catholic Church is al-together independent of the Bible."[12]

This attitude is based on the historic Roman Catholic hostility to the general reading of the Bible as expressed by many popes and church councils. Pope Pius VII, for instance, in 1816, denounced Bible Societies as "a crafty device by which the very foundations of religion are undermined, a pestilence which must be remedied and abolished." And Pope Leo XIII, in 1897, prohibited "all versions in any vernacular language made by non-Catholics, and specially those published by the Bible Societies."

It is denied by the hierarchy and by many Roman Catholics today that the Roman Catholic church is against the general reading of the Bible. But those who con-scientiously try to place Bibles and Testaments and even copies of the Gospels in schools and hotels and homes testify to the constant opposition and incredible pressures exerted by Roman Catholics, on school boards and else-where, to the placement of Bibles for general reading.

It is only natural, however, that the Roman Cath-olic church should continue to fight with all her resources the general reading of the Bible. For the priests know full well that an open Bible is an open refutation of the whole Roman Catholic system—with its man-made traditions, its superstitions, and its Christ-dishonoring rituals. The Roman Catholic hierarchy has always known—and has consistently and ruthlessly operated on that knowledge—that an open Bible is the greatest enemy of the Roman Catholic church, and that it is the most effective refutation of the hierarchy's fantastic claims.

III. What Do Roman Catholics Believe About Salvation?

To Roman Catholics, who do not believe in direct access to God, but believe that they must go through intermediaries—the agency of the church, the priests, the Virgin Mary, and the saints—salvation is gained by observance of the sacraments and regulations of the Roman Catholic church.

A sacrament, to a Roman Catholic, is an external sign, instituted by Christ, which works automatically— "of itself"—for the mediating of the grace of God to the soul of man. There are seven sacraments in the Roman Catholic church: baptism, confirmation, the Eucharist, penance, extreme unction, matrimony, and ordination. Since the last two are of necessity for special groups only, the first five are the sacraments absolutely necessary to salvation.

To understand what a Roman Catholic believes about salvation, however, one must know what the Roman Catholic teaching is concerning sin. Roman Catholics believe in original sin. They also believe that the sins a person commits are the *willful* thoughts, words, deeds, and omissions which are contrary to the law of God, and that these sins fall into two categories: venial and mortal. Venial sin is the less serious of the two and can be atoned for in this life or in purgatory. Mortal sin, however, is so serious that one would have to spend eternity in hell, unless the punishment is taken away by God's grace.

In the sacrament of baptism a Roman Catholic believes that original sin is washed away, and that both mortal and venial sins committed prior to baptism are remitted, or blotted out, and that the grace of regeneration is then bestowed. Baptism is administered to both infants and adults by pouring, and all baptized persons are then listed as members of the church.

In the sacrament of confirmation the bishop, who alone can confirm, makes the sign of the cross on the person's brow, anoints with oil, slaps the person lightly on the cheek, and lays his hands on him. The use of oil and the laying on of hands indicate the baptism of the Holy Spirit, and the slap on the cheek is a reminder that suffering is the lot of Christians.

In the sacrament of the Eucharist (which is not to be confused with the Mass, wherein the priest bloodlessly sacrifices Christ afresh on the altar) a person partakes, after the sacrifice of the Mass, of the consecrated element (the bread) and thereby receives Christ—His body and His blood. This sacrament remits venial sin, but does not necessarily remit the punishment of the sin.

In the sacrament of penance the person who commits a mortal sin after baptism makes "satisfaction"—the doing of some meritorious act prescribed by the priest—and is "absolved" by the priest. This sacrament of penance, however, must always be preceded by a full confession to the priest of the sin. Confession is made in the "confessional," a small booth of two compartments with a small screen between; on one side is the priest and on the other side the one making the confession, but they cannot see each other. The primary function of the sacrament of penance is to forgive mortal sin and to take away *eternal* punishment—this sacrament keeps one from going to hell.

It is here, at this point of confession and absolution, that the priest exerts his greatest authority over the Roman Catholic. For a Roman Catholic believes that there is no forgiveness for sins unless mediated through the priest—and the priests have for centuries carefully and cleverly built up a whole diabolical system of fear and superstition and greed by a distortion of the statement of Jesus to His disciples: "Whose soever sins ye remit, they are remitted unto them; and whose soever sins ye retain, they are retained" (John 20:23).

There is no record in the entire New Testament that the disciples understood Jesus to mean that they were to have authority to forgive men of sins, and the whole idea of the confessional and penance was foreign to the Early Church. In fact, it was not until A.D. 1215 that the Roman church, through Pope Innocent III, made auricular confession an article of faith. But this Christ-discrediting belief has so fastened itself upon the minds of Roman Catholics that they actually believe the fantastic words of one of their priests when he says in a catechism:

> Q. Are Protestants willing to confess their sins to a Catholic bishop or priest, who alone has power from Christ to forgive sins?
> A. No, for they generally have an aversion to confession, and therefore their sins will not be forgiven them throughout all eternity.
> Q. What follows from this?
> A. That they die in their sins and are damned.

How incredible that men will believe this lie when they have the privilege of believing God's Word when it says:

If we confess our sins, he [God] is faithful and just to forgive us our sins, and to cleanse us from all unrighteousness (I John 1:9);

and,

Let the wicked forsake his way, and the unrighteous man his thoughts: and let him return unto the Lord, and he will have mercy upon him; and to our God, for he will abundantly pardon (Isa. 55:7).

In the sacrament of extreme unction the priest goes to a person who is dangerously ill and thought to be dying, and anoints him with holy oil—olive oil which has been blessed. With the tip of his finger the priest places a small amount of the oil on the lids of the eyes, the lobes of the ears, the nostrils, the lips, the hands, and the feet. While he does this he says:

> Through this holy unction and His most tender mercy may the Lord pardon thee whatever sins or faults thou hast committed by sight, hearing, smell, taste, touch, and walking.

And this, like all other sacraments, so a Roman Catholic believes, confers grace through the infinite merits of Christ, and takes care of any sins not previously forgiven.

WHAT DO ROMAN CATHOLICS BELIEVE ABOUT PURGATORY?

It would seem that with all the elaborate ritual of the sacraments, a Roman Catholic would at last be ready for heaven, but such is not the case. There is "purgatory" to think about—and to suffer through.

Purgatory is a word that cannot be found in the Bible, and the idea it conveys is absolutely foreign to the Scriptures, but to a Roman Catholic it is a very definite and important stage in the plan of salvation.

According to the Roman Catholic *Baltimore Catechism:*

> Purgatory is the state in which those suffer for a time who die guilty of venial sins, or without having satisfied for the punishment due to their sins.

It is the place, or state, where souls suffer torment to atone for the sins they have committed on earth. And everyone—good and bad, saint and sinner—has to endure, for a time, the torture of the fires of purgatory. When the last pope died, for instance, the whole Roman Catholic world prayed fervently that he would have a speedy passage through purgatory. But no one knows just how long anyone has to endure the torment of purgatory.

Roman Catholics believe, however, that the punishment of purgatory will have an end and that every soul will be released as soon as its debt for sin has been paid. Furthermore, purgatory itself will one day cease to exist. This discussion of purgatory will be continued in the answer to the question about future life, but this much is included here because, to a Roman Catholic, salvation cannot be completed without the cleansing and punishing fires of purgatory.

What Do Roman Catholics Believe About Indulgences?

Believing in a priest-invented purgatory, a Roman Catholic is very grateful for the Roman Catholic teaching of "indulgence." This, in effect, is a priest-concocted method of increasing the authority of the clergy and the church over the laity. An indulgence is the remission of a certain amount of temporal punishment which remains due to sin, thereby reducing one's time, or one's pain, in purgatory.

Indulgences may be granted for offering certain prayers, going on pilgrimages to sacred shrines, and making donations to Roman Catholic causes. The pope, so a Roman Catholic believes, has access to the "treasury of merit," which is the "treasury" or "storehouse" filled with the excess merits of Christ and the Virgin Mary and the saints of the church, and is thus able to put some of these excess merits to the credit of the person who performs a meritorious deed, thereby shortening his time or pain in purgatory.

One can readily see the incredible influence and authority this Roman Catholic belief gives to the clergy, and also the almost unlimited opportunities for graft and corruption. In reality, an indulgence, as it has been generally practiced in the Roman Catholic church, is just a religious "shakedown" for a supposedly good cause. And it was this "shakedown," this graft and this corruption of indulgences, which helped to bring on the Reformation.

For early in the sixteenth century, a clever and crafty Roman Catholic priest by the name of John Tetzel was sent by the pope into parts of Germany to oversee the selling of indulgences in order to help enlarge the Church of St. Peter in Rome, and to "pay off" a banker by the name of John Fugger for money he had loaned to help "buy" an archbishopric for Albert of Brandenburg. This traffic in indulgences became so corrupt that Martin Luther finally objected so strenuously that in the ensuing conflict he felt it necessary to publish his views. So on October 31, 1517, he nailed his ninety-five theses concerning indulgences on the door of the Wittenberg church, and the Reformation was on.

The belief in indulgences, however, and the graft that goes with them, still continue to this day in the Roman Catholic church, the only difference being that today the excesses are more polished and the extortion and "shakedown" are more subtle and much more refined than in the days of Tetzel.

WHAT ARE "SUFFRAGES"?

While an indulgence is obtained to shorten one's own time in purgatory, a "suffrage" is an indulgence secured on the behalf of a deceased person to shorten *his* term in purgatory. Thus a living Roman Catholic can pray for a dead loved one or friend, pay a priest to say Masses for the deceased, and apply various indulgences to his credit. But again, no one knows for sure whether the suffrage, or merit of it, will actually shorten the deceased person's time in purgatory; one only "hopes" or "piously believes" that it will.

No one could even begin to estimate the human misery and suffering caused by this priest-promoted belief in "suffrages." Roman Catholic priests for centuries have held this heavy club over the heads of ignorant and superstitious members, draining them of their money and human energies to "pay" for a deceased loved one's easy and shortened passage through purgatory.

The whole crafty scheme is nothing less than extortion and is an absolute denial of the clear teachings of the Bible and spirit of Christ. What a "vicar of Christ," what a "priest of the most high God"—so hard and so calloused and so insensitive that he would have to be *paid* to ease the pains, or shorten the time, of a poor soul suffering the tormenting flames of "purgatory"!

Salvation, then, to a Roman Catholic, consists of the whole elaborate array of sacraments—the cleansing of baptism, the Holy Spirit bestowed in confirmation, the forgiveness of venial sins through the Eucharist, and of mortal sins through confession and penance, and the final forgiveness in extreme unction; then the suffering in purgatory and finally, after the debt is fully paid, bliss in heaven.[13]

There is no certainty, no assurance, no witness of the Spirit to salvation in Roman Catholic teaching. Even the pope himself has his own confessor to whom he confesses his sins and is "absolved."

How much simpler, how scriptural and Christ-honoring it is to accept salvation according to *God's* plan: "Whosoever shall call upon the name of the Lord shall be saved" (Rom. 10:13)!

IV. What Do Roman Catholics Believe About the Future Life?

Because of the involved Roman Catholic teaching of salvation it was necessary to briefly discuss the Roman teaching of the future life under the question of salvation. But, more specifically, Roman Catholics believe that there are four possible places (or states) for the soul after death: purgatory, limbo, heaven, or hell.

As was seen above, a Roman Catholic believes that everyone at death goes to purgatory, there to suffer the temporal punishment for sins—even though the guilt of those sins may have been removed by a priest of the Roman Catholic church. But Jesus, in His promise to the thief on the cross, did not say anything about purgatory. He did say, "To day shalt thou be with me in paradise" (Luke 23:43). The whole idea of purgatory is a fabrication of greedy men and is a direct denial of the Scriptures.

Limbo is an abode of natural happiness where souls went if they were justified before Christ, at His resurrection, opened the gates of heaven. The saints of the Old Testament, for example, went to limbo. Unbaptized infants also go to limbo. It is a place of much greater natural happiness than the earth.[14]

Heaven, to a Roman Catholic, is a definite place—a place where those souls go who have paid the full penalty for sins and have been made pure in the fires of purgatory, and where they experience a supernatural happiness. At the last day, Roman Catholics believe, the souls in heaven will receive back their bodies. These bodies will be glorified and will be immortal, and will be beyond the reach of pain and incapable of sin forever.

Hell, as conceived by a Roman Catholic, is a place or state where the damned—demons and unbaptized and willfully evil men—are punished eternally for their sins.

A Roman Catholic believes that if a person *willfully* rejects the claims of the Roman Catholic church as being the only *true* church, and deliberately refuses to avail himself of the sacraments of the Roman Catholic church and lives in willful disobedience to her rules and regulations, that person will be damned and will spend eternity in the flames of hell.

Why, then, am I a Nazarene and not a Roman Catholic?

1. I am not a Roman Catholic because, as a Nazarene, I believe that the Church of Christ is made up of all born-again Christians—

For as the body is one, and hath many members, and all the members of that one body, being many, are one body: so also is Christ. For by one Spirit are we all baptized into one body, . . . whether we be bond or free; and have been all made to drink into one Spirit (I Cor. 12:12-13),

and so I could never believe the fantastic claims of the Roman Catholic church that *it* is the only "true" church and that all who are willfully and knowingly outside its folds are deceived and will ultimately be damned.

2. I am not a Roman Catholic because, as a Nazarene, I believe that Christ himself is the Head of His Church—

And he is the head of the body, the church: who is the beginning, the firstborn from the dead; that in all things he might have the preeminence (Col. 1:18),

and so I could never believe the Christ-dishonoring teaching of the Roman Catholic church that the pope in Rome is "infallible" and is the "head of the church" and the "vicar of Christ" on earth.

3. I am not a Roman Catholic because, as a Nazarene, I believe in the priesthood of all believers and

that Christ and Christ alone is the Intermediary between man and God—

For there is one God, and one mediator between God and men, the man Christ Jesus (I Tim. 2:5); and, *We have an advocate with the Father, Jesus Christ the righteous* (I John 2:1),

and so I could never believe in the "cult of Mary" and the "Mariolatry" of the Roman Catholic church, which makes Mary more merciful than Christ, and the saints more attentive to human need than is our blessed Lord.

4. I am not a Roman Catholic because, as a Nazarene, I believe that when Christ died on the Cross He died once for all—

And every priest standeth daily ministering and offering oftentimes the same sacrifices, which can never take away sins: but this man, after he had offered one sacrifice for sins for ever, sat down on the right hand of God (Heb. 10:11-12),

and so I could never believe in the incredible heresy of the Roman Catholic church that every time a Roman Catholic priest says the Mass, Christ is crucified afresh on that Roman Catholic altar.

5. I am not a Roman Catholic because, as a Nazarene, I believe that the observance of the Lord's Supper is a symbolic remembrance of Christ's death—

And when he had given thanks, he brake it, and said, Take, eat: this is my body, which is broken for you: this do in remembrance of me (I Cor. 11:24),

and so I could never believe the fantastic claims of the Roman Catholic church that her priests are mysteriously able to change common bread and wine into the actual flesh and blood of Jesus Christ.

6. I am not a Roman Catholic because, as a Nazarene, I believe the Bible to be a sufficient and adequate guide as it is interpreted by the Holy Spirit—

Howbeit in vain do they worship me, teaching for doctrines the commandments of men. For laying aside the commandment of God, ye hold the tradition of men, as the washing of pots and cups: and many other such like things ye do. And he said unto them, Full well ye reject the commandment of God, that ye may keep your own tradition (Mark 7:7-9); and,

Howbeit when he, the Spirit of truth, is come, he will guide you into all truth: for he shall not speak of himself, but whatsoever he shall hear, that shall he speak: and he will shew you things to come (John 16:13),

and so I could never believe the Bible-dishonoring and Holy Ghost-discrediting teaching that the traditions of the Roman Catholic church are equal in authority to the inspired and sacred Scriptures and that the Roman church is the only safe guide and interpreter of the Bible.

7. I am not a Roman Catholic because, as a Nazarene, I believe that only God can forgive sin—

To the Lord our God belong mercies and forgivenesses, though we have rebelled against him (Dan. 9:9); and,

Let the wicked forsake his way, and the unrighteous man his thoughts: and let him return unto the Lord, and he will have mercy upon him; and to our God, for he will abundantly pardon (Isa. 55:7),

and so I could never believe that a mere Roman Catholic priest, by some religious magic or hocus-pocus, has the power to absolve and forgive men of their sins.

8. I am not a Roman Catholic because, as a Nazarene, I believe that original sin is cleansed from the

human heart by the baptism with the Holy Ghost and fire—

I indeed baptize you with water unto repentance: but he that cometh after me is mightier than I, whose shoes I am not worthy to bear: he shall baptize you with the Holy Ghost, and with fire (Matt. 3:11);

and,

God, which knoweth the hearts, bare them witness, giving them the Holy Ghost, even as he did unto us; and put no difference between us and them, purifying their hearts by faith (Acts 15:8-9),

and so I could never believe the Roman Catholic doctrine that in the sacrament of water baptism original sin is cleansed from the human heart.

9. I am not a Roman Catholic because, as a Nazarene, I believe that the souls of the righteous go immediately at death to be with the Lord in paradise—

Blessed are the dead which die in the Lord from henceforth: Yea, saith the Spirit, that they may rest from their labours (Rev. 14:13),

and so I could never believe in the priest-invented purgatory nor in the callous and greedy religious extortion of indulgences and suffrages.

10. I am not a Roman Catholic because, as a Nazarene, I believe in freedom and liberty—

Now therefore why tempt ye God, to put a yoke upon the neck of the disciples, which neither our fathers nor we were able to bear? (Acts 15:10);

and,

If the Son therefore shall make you free, ye shall be free indeed (John 8:36),

and so I could never believe in the totalitarian system of the Roman Catholic church which decries totalitarian-

ism in politics but practices it in religion, and denies freedom to those who disagree with its Bible-distorting doctrines in those countries where it is in the majority, and is guilty of ever-encroaching limitation of liberty in those countries where it is in the minority.

Those countries of the world that are most Roman Catholic are those most ignorant and most enslaved; those countries of the world that are most Protestant are those enjoying the highest standard of education and the greatest measure of liberty and freedom.

This people draweth nigh unto me with their mouth, and honoureth me with their lips; but their heart is far from me. But in vain they do worship me, teaching for doctrines the commandments of men.

—Matt. 15:8-9

Chapter Four

WHY I AM A NAZARENE

and Not a Jehovah's Witness

WHAT IS A JEHOVAH'S WITNESS?

It is difficult to give an exact definition of a Jehovah's Witness. Even Marley Cole, a non-Witness apologist, says: "A precise definition of Jehovah's Witnesses is not easily arrived at."[1] It can be said, however, that a Jehovah's Witness is one who has become a minister, or "publisher," of the Watchtower Bible and Tract Society, and who devotes incredible time and urgent energy to preaching the Society's distorted interpretations of Bible prophecy.

WHERE DO JEHOVAH'S WITNESSES GET THEIR NAME?

They were not known as "Jehovah's Witnesses" until 1931. Before that time they were known variously as "The Millennial Dawnists," "The International Bible Students," and, earlier, "Russellites."

The name Jehovah's Witnesses was officially adopted at Columbus, Ohio, in 1931, at the suggestion of the then head of the movement, Judge J. F. Rutherford, who said: "By the grace of the Lord Jesus Christ and of our heavenly Father, we joyfully receive and bear the name which the mouth of Jehovah God has named and given us, to wit, Jehovah's Witnesses."[2]

Among the reasons for the adoption of that name, as stated in the *Watchtower,* was that "Jesus Christ calls himself the faithful and true Witness . . . Jesus must necessarily be Jehovah's Witness, his Chief Witness. Imitators and followers of Jesus, to be Christians, would have to be Jehovah's Witnesses."[3] And then Rutherford adds the words of Isa. 43:10: "Ye are my witnesses, saith Jehovah."

The real reason for the change of name, however, was the felt necessity to divorce the organization from the excesses and accretions of Russellism, and to distinguish Rutherford's group from various splinter groups of Russellites, the most important of which being the "Dawnists," who, incidentally, now sponsor the coast-to-coast radio program "Frank and Ernest."

WHO WAS THE FOUNDER OF JEHOVAH'S WITNESSES?

Most Jehovah's Witnesses will get highly indignant if it is suggested that their cult had a "human" founder. Judge Rutherford claimed that the Witnesses had been on earth as an organization for more than 5,000 years, and cited Hebrews 11 to prove it.

Charles Taze Russell, however, was the founder and first president of what is now Jehovah's Witnesses. Born February 16, 1852, young Russell spent most of his early years in Pittsburgh and Allegheny County, Pennsylvania. In 1870, at the age of eighteen, Russell organized a Bible class in Pittsburgh, which in 1876 elected him "pastor" of the group. In 1879 "Pastor" Russell founded *Zion's Watchtower*, which is known today as *The Watchtower Announcing Jehovah's Kingdom*. The year 1884 marks the beginning of the organization now known as Jehovah's Witnesses, for it was in that year that Charles Taze Russell founded the religious organization named the "Zion's Watchtower Society," and from that humble beginning "Pastor" Russell saw his movement grow and expand, under a succession of names, until before his death in 1916 he had girdled the globe and perverted the minds of thousands with his pernicious doctrines.

Much has been written of the disreputable character of "Pastor" Russell: his outright perjury on the witness stand when he claimed he could read Greek and then had to admit that he couldn't even identify a letter of the Greek alphabet . . . his imprudent relationship with women, particularly a young servant girl in his home . . . his attempt to cheat his own wife out of money rightfully belonging to her, and his fraudulent practices in handling money coming to the "Society" . . . his being divorced because of his wayward affections and deceitful ways . . . his widely publicized financial fiasco in trying to sell "miracle" wheat to the faithful at sixty dollars a bushel . . . his arrogant conceit in saying that it would be better for a person to leave the Bible unopened and to read his own *Studies in the Scriptures* than to fail to read them and read only the Bible . . . his open claim that he was an ordained minister, which he had to deny when faced in court with the evidence that he had never been ordained by anybody, anywhere.

Need more be said to convince those who search for truth that Charles Taze Russell was one of the most disreputable religious racketeers and frauds ever to pervert the faith and destroy the confidence of sincere believers? How much better it would have been, for Christianity and for the world, if "Pastor" Russell had continued as a haberdasher, in which role he did well, instead of becoming a religious charlatan, in which role he did untold damage to the minds and souls of millions.

And yet this is the man of whom his colleague and successor, Judge Rutherford, said: "When the history of the Church of Christ is fully written, it will be found that the place next to St. Paul in the gallery of fame as expounders of the Gospel of the great Master will be occupied by Charles Taze Russell."[4] And this is the man whom the Witnesses regard as "the foremost human pioneer in doctrinal reformation more far-reaching and more important to posterity than anything that had been done since the days of Jesus and the apostles."[5]

And this is the man—in all his quirks, conceits, ignorance, arrogance, and shams—this bearded Elmer Gantry—this is the man who founded, and whose weird "theology" guides, the frenzied faith and frantic efforts of over six hundred thousand Jehovah's Witnesses around the world.

Who Have Been the Leaders of Jehovah's Witnesses Since Russell?

Upon "Pastor" Russell's death, October 31, 1916, the overwhelming majority of the Witnesses turned to Judge Joseph Franklin Rutherford for leadership. He had made himself popular with Russell for his work as legal adviser to the Society, and to the Witnesses at large by his vicious attacks on "organized religion." Judge Rutherford's legal experience (he had served briefly in his earlier years as special judge of the Eighth Judicial Circuit Court of Boonville, Missouri)[6] was to serve him well in his many skirmishes within the organization and his many battles with "unbelievers."

His legal experience, however, did not save him from serving a term in the Atlanta Federal Penitentiary for violation of the "Espionage Act" in 1918. But when he was released from prison in 1919 he returned to the Witnesses as a martyr-hero. And he continued to rule the Witnesses with an iron hand until his death at his palatial mansion, "Beth Sarim," in San Diego, California, January 8, 1942. He was seventy-two when he died.

Judge Rutherford's contribution to the Jehovah's Witnesses was considerable. He it was who initiated radio talks and the use of phonograph recordings as important adjuncts to the proselytizing zeal of the Witnesses. Over one hundred books and pamphlets came from his pen, and his writings have been translated into over eighty languages around the world.

When Judge Rutherford died, Nathan H. Knorr was elected president of the organization. Even though he has served in that top position since 1942, little is known about him, as he surrounds himself with secrecy. He works hard at the Witness headquarters in Brooklyn, refuses all but a few requests for interviews, and appears mainly at the great International Conventions of Jehovah's Witnesses, where in 1953 he spoke to over 170,-000 in and around Yankee Stadium and the Polo Grounds in New York City.

Marcus Bach, a very charitable and objective researcher in the religions of America, evaluates the leadership of the Jehovah's Witnesses as follows: "Scandal surrounded Pastor Russell; mystery, Judge Rutherford; silence, Brother Knorr."[7]

Do JEHOVAH'S WITNESSES REALLY HATE THE CHURCHES?

Stanley High, writing in the *Saturday Evening Post* for September 14, 1940, said: "Jehovah's Witnesses hate everybody and try to make it mutual." It has been said that the Jehovah's Witnesses actually make hate a religion. Their "purest" hatred (and they actually distinguish between ordinary hate and "pure" hate), however, is reserved for the churches, which they call "enemies of God" and "instruments of the Devil." As Rutherford said, "Religion is of the Devil."[8] And the Witnesses never hesitate to make "religion" and "churches" synonomous.

Another Witness writer declares:

> The mask is down, the truth of God's Word has ripped it off and organized religion (the churches) stands exposed as being not of the Lord God and Christ but of their enemy, Satan—the Devil. It stands stripped of its Christian

professions and stands naked as being demonism! Religion is revealed as the unchangeable foe of Christianity.[9]

If anyone is still in doubt as to what Jehovah's Witnesses really think about the Church, these words of Judge Rutherford's should clarify the matter:

> These facts are set forth here, not for the purpose of holding men up to ridicule, but for the purpose of informing the people that the ecclesiastical systems, Catholic and Protestant, are under supervision and control of the Devil, and form a part of his visible organization, and therefore constitute the anti-Christ.[10]

Why Do Jehovah's Witnesses Refuse to Salute the Flag?

There are millions of Americans who know nothing of the dangerous doctrines believed by Jehovah's Witnesses, who are yet opposed, in varying degrees of intensity, to all the Witnesses because of their refusal to serve in the armed services of their country and their refusal to salute the flag. And in test cases before the United States Supreme Court, the Witnesses have won the right to refuse both.

Their reason for refusing such obviously patriotic duties and privileges is the claim that to salute the flag would be an act of idolatry:

> Jehovah's Witnesses do not salute the flag of any nation. . . . Their position world-wide on this issue is a scriptural one. . . . Any national flag is a symbol or image of the sovereign power of that nation. . . . The giving of the salute to the flag of any nation is an act that ascribes salvation to the flag and to the nation for which it stands.
>
> Therefore, no Witness of Jehovah, who ascribes salvation *only* to Him, may salute any flag of any nation without a violation of Jehovah's commandment against idolatry as stated in His word.[11]

And yet the Witnesses have no hesitation whatsoever in appealing to the very courts and organizations of world governments which, they claim, are "demon controlled." Neither do the Witnesses hesitate to enjoy the freedoms that their patriotic neighbors have purchased for them through sacrifice and blood.

I. What Do Jehovah's Witnesses Believe About Christ?

For one thing, *they deny His deity*. "Pastor" Russell wrote:

> When Jesus was in the flesh, he was a perfect human being: previous to that time he was a perfect spiritual being. Since his resurrection he is a perfect spiritual being of the highest or Divine Order. . . . It was not until the time of his consecration, even unto death, as typified in baptism at thirty years of age, that he received the earnest of his inheritance of the divine nature.[12]

Russell denied that Christ was both human and divine when He was upon the earth:

> Neither was Jesus a combination of two natures, human and spiritual. The blending of two natures produces neither the one nor the other, but an imperfect hybrid thing, which is obnoxious to the divine arrangement.[13]

To Russell, Jesus Christ was nothing more than a created angel:

> Our Redeemer existed as a spirit being before He was made flesh and dwelt amongst men. At that time, as well as subsequently, he was properly known as a "god"—a mighty one. As chief of the angels, and next to the Father, he was known as the Archangel (highest angel or messenger) whose name, Michael, signified, "Who as God," or God's representative.[14]

The flat denial of the deity of Jesus Christ is made in the Witness book *Reconciliation:* "Jesus was not God the Son."[15] And also in their book *Let God Be True:* "The truth of the matter is that the *word* is Christ Jesus, who did have a beginning."[16] And again, "If Jesus were

God, then during Jesus' death God was dead and in the grave."[17]

In case anyone is still in doubt that the Jehovah's Witnesses deny the deity of Christ, Judge Rutherford erases that doubt completely when he says:

> Some have earnestly believed that Jesus was God himself. But such a conclusion is not warranted by Scripture.[18] . . . Some insist that Jesus when on earth was both God and man in completeness. This theory is wrong, however. . . . It is also easy to be seen that Jesus could not be part God and part man, because that would be more than the law required; hence divine justice could not accept such a ransom.[19]

This, then, is the Christ of Jehovah's Witnesses—an angel, a messenger, a representative, a created being, a perfect man, but *not* the only begotten Son of God, the God-Man, in whom "dwelleth all the fulness of the Godhead bodily."

For another thing, *Jehovah's Witnesses deny the physical resurrection of Christ*. Russell was very explicit in his denial of the bodily resurrection of Christ:

> Our Lord's human body was, however, supernaturally removed from the tomb; because had it remained there it would have been an insurmountable obstacle to the faith of the disciples. . . . We know nothing about what became of it . . . Whether it was dissolved into gases or whether it is still preserved somewhere as the grand memorial of God's love, no one knows.[20]

And with continued falsehood Russell says:

> Jesus at and after his resurrection was a spirit—a spirit being of the highest order of the divine nature. . . . was put to death a man, but was raised from the dead a spirit being of the highest order of the divine nature. . . . The man Jesus is dead, forever dead.[22]

Rutherford continues this incredible teaching by declaring:

> Our Lord's human body, the one crucified, was re-
> moved from the tomb by the power of God. . . . The Scrip-
> ture does not reveal what became of the body except that
> it did not decay or corrupt . . . The Scriptures tell us
> that God miraculously hid the body of Moses; and Jehovah
> could just as easily have preserved and hid away the body
> of Jesus.[23]

How is it possible for anyone—Jehovah's Witness or
anyone else—to actually believe these outrageous denials
when God's Word clearly says that Jesus appeared before His disciples after His resurrection and as He "stood
in the midst of them, . . . he said unto them, Why are
ye troubled? and why do thoughts arise in your hearts?
Behold my hands and my feet, that it is I myself; handle
me, and see; for a spirit hath not flesh and bones, as ye
see me have. And when he had thus spoken, he shewed
them his hands and his feet. And while they yet believed
not for joy, and wondered, he said unto them, Have ye
here any meat? And they gave him a piece of a broiled
fish, and of an honeycomb. And he took it, and did eat
before them"?[24]

*Jehovah's Witnesses also deny the bodily return of
Jesus Christ.* On this important point "Pastor" Russell
says:

> We must bear in mind, also, that our Lord is no longer
> a human being . . . Since he is no longer in any sense or
> degree a human being, we must not expect him to come
> again as a human being.[25]

The plain teaching of the Scriptures is totally dis-
regarded by the Witnesses when they say:

> Some wrongfully expect a literal fulfillment of the
> symbolic statements of the Bible. Such hope to see the
> glorified Jesus coming seated on a white cloud where
> every human eye will see him. Since no earthly men have
> ever seen the Father . . . neither will they see the glori-
> fied Son.

Seeing, then, that Jehovah's Witnesses reject and emphatically deny the deity of Jesus Christ, His physical resurrection and return to earth, whatever else might be said about them, it must be said, in kindness but in honesty, that they are not Christian, for John clearly warns us:

Every spirit that confesseth not that Jesus Christ is come in the flesh is not of God: and this is that spirit of antichrist, whereof ye have heard that it should come; and even now already is it in the world (I John 4:3).

II. WHAT DO JEHOVAH'S WITNESSES BELIEVE ABOUT THE BIBLE?

Jehovah's Witnesses are very proud of the fact that they are able to quote scripture on almost any conceivable subject. In this, as in almost everything else, "Pastor" Russell set the pattern, for it is said that there are over 5,000 scripture quotations in his volumes of *Studies in the Scriptures.*

As is true with all cults, however, Jehovah's Witnesses do not accept the Bible "as is"—there are other books which "supplement" the Bible, and which must be read along with the Bible if one is to get the "truth." Chief among these "supplements" are Russell's own *Studies in the Scriptures,* which he himself admitted were so necessary to the understanding of the Bible that, if one could not read both the Bible and his *Studies,* it would be far better to leave the Bible unread and to read only the *Studies in the Scriptures.*

Russell's followers have shared his conceit by saying:

If the six volumes of *Scripture Studies* are practically the Bible, topically arranged with Bible proof texts given, we might not improperly name the volumes, "The Bible in an Arranged Form." That is to say, they are not mere comments on the Bible, but they are practically the Bible itself. Furthermore, not only do we find that people cannot see the divine plan in studying the Bible itself, but we see, also, that if anyone lays the *Scripture Studies* aside, even after he has used them, after he has become familiar with them, after he has read them for ten years—if he then lays them aside and ignores them and goes to the Bible alone, though he has understood his Bible for ten years, our experience shows that within two years he goes into darkness. On the other hand, if he had merely read the *Scripture Studies* with their references and had not read a page of the Bible as such, he would be in the light at the end of two years, because he would then have the light of the Scriptures.[26]

The present Jehovah's Witnesses, however, go far beyond Russell and his earlier followers in their attitude toward the Bible. For they not only insist on the "supplements" to the Bible; the present Jehovah's Witnesses have *changed* the Bible to read the way they want it to read, so that they can quote the Bible to substantiate their perverted and twisted doctrines.

This newest attempt at distorting what the Bible really teaches is by means of *new translations* of the Bible called *The New World Translation of the Christian Greek Scriptures*, containing the entire New Testament, and *The New World Translation of the Hebrew Scriptures*, containing, at present, the first seventeen books of the Old Testament.

These *new translations* were first published in 1950 and later revised in 1951. They have already had phenomenal sale among the Witnesses but they only prove once again that "Jehovah's Witnesses are only interested in what they can make the Scriptures say, and not in what the Holy Spirit has already perfectly revealed."[27] And, as Peter warned, these translators "wrest . . . the . . . scriptures to their own destruction"[28]—*and* the destruction of those who read and believe their pernicious perversions of the Holy Bible.

III. What Do Jehovah's Witnesses Believe About Salvation?

Salvation, to the Jehovah's Witnesses, largely consists in being "imitators" of Jesus, which is, of course, self-salvation, and is nothing more than justification by works rather than justification by faith.

By believing that Jesus was only a man until His resurrection, the Witnesses nullify the redemptive plan and power of the cross of Christ. For if Jesus was only "perfect man" until His resurrection—when He arose "an invisible spirit creature"—then there was no deity at the Cross, and the blood spilled on Calvary is only that of mere man and so cannot be efficacious for the remission of sins or for that cleansing which can be effected only through the blood of God's own Son.

While denying the deity of Jesus Christ and making the Cross of no effect, the Witnesses claim that all Jesus did by dying was to pay the "ransom" necessary to set men free from death, so they could have a second chance. As Russell expressed it:

> The "ransom for all" given by "the man Christ Jesus" does not give or guarantee everlasting life or blessing to any man; but it does guarantee to every man another opportunity or trial for life everlasting.[29]

Jehovah's Witnesses know nothing of conversion, or regeneration, or justification by faith, or cleansing from sin, or the baptism with the Holy Ghost, or being filled with the Spirit. These words, and the experiences they signify, are foreign to their faith and foreign to their vocabulary. In fact, in denying that the redeeming work of Christ was completed on the Cross, it is impossible for them to ever know Him in saving grace. And by denying the reality of the Holy Spirit as a Person—"The Holy Spirit is not a person in the Godhead"[30] . . . "There is no personal Holy Spirit revealed in the Scriptures"[31] —the Witnesses make it forever impossible to know what it means to be "saved" and "sanctified." Pentecost is meaningless to a Jehovah's Witness.

The Jehovah's Witnesses would rather believe "Pastor" Russell's Christ-denying doctrine that each must work out his own salvation than the Apostle Paul's glad proclamation, "By grace are ye saved through faith; and that not of yourselves: it is the gift of God: not of works, lest any man should boast" (Eph. 2:8-9).

A Jehovah's Witness never knows the joyous thrill of having the Spirit himself bear witness that he is the child of God. And those who believe the Holy Spirit to be nothing more than an "impersonal influence" can never know the blessed joy and radiant victory of being "filled with the Spirit."

In view of the Jehovah's Witnesses Christ-denying, Spirit-denying, Blood-denying plan of "salvation," it is not too much to say, with Dr. Dixon, "Its plan of Salvation is a plan of damnation."

IV. What Do Jehovah's Witnesses Believe About the Future Life?

Before one can even begin to understand the Jehovah's Witnesses' weird and distorted doctrines concerning the future life, one must understand something of what they mean by death.

Death, to Jehovah's Witnesses, means *extinction,* the cessation of being, annihilation. Russell himself gives this theory expression when he says:

> Death is a period of absolute unconsciousness—more than that it is a period of absolute non-existence.[32] . . . Our Lord's being or soul was non-existent during the period of death. . . . It was necessary, not only that the man Christ Jesus should die, but just as necessary that the man Christ Jesus should never live again, should remain dead to all eternity.[33]

The same twisted thinking is expressed by Rutherford when he says:

> Another of Satan's deceptions by which he has blinded the people is the teaching that the dead are still conscious after death. . . . Those who die are never conscious again. . . . Man was made out of dust. He was sentenced to return to the dust.[34]

So to Jehovah's Witnesses, death has but one meaning: complete destruction—total and absolute; annihilation—complete and without qualification.

And what do they do with the many scriptures that teach consciousness after death? Their "explanation" of Christ's remark to the thief on the cross will serve as an example of their shifty evasions. Rutherford explains it this way:

> The thief will never be in heaven, because the promise to him is that if he is on the side of Christ Jesus he will be in paradise. It is certain that the thief did not go to heaven or paradise that day that he died. If he did, then he got there long before Jesus did. . . . The thief died and was put in the grave and is still in the grave. . . . The words of Jesus to the thief were these: "Today I say unto thee (that is, I am saying it now, this day), shalt thou be with me in paradise?"[35]

What a sinister system—that will evade the clear teaching of God's Word by a change of punctuation! God's Word says: "To day shalt thou be with me in paradise."[36]

Of all the warped and twisted theories in the Jehovah's Witness system, the most distorted, the most unscriptural—and the most appealing to the wicked—is the doctrine described as "no hellism." Jehovah's Witnesses totally reject the scriptural teaching of eternal punishment. Russell not only rejects it; he ridicules it.

In his comments on Mark 9: 47-48, Russell says:

> This text has long been a favorite with the hellfire screechers. In it they think they have conclusive proof

that the sinners are punished by torment in a fire which is never quenched. They argue with great warmth that the worms die not. But be it noted that the only thing mentioned as dying not are worms. Therefore, it is the worms that are immortal, from their viewpoint. Nothing is said about human beings as alive and conscious in that fire.[37] . . . Eternal torture is nowhere taught in the Bible.[38]

Judge Rutherford adds his "me too" by saying:

The doctrine of eternal torment was never heard of for more than four thousand years after Adam was sentenced to death. It is an invention of the Devil . . . for supporting . . . his original lie: namely, that there is no death. . . . The doctrines of eternal torture and inherent immortality are intended to support each other and both being false, both must fall.[39]

That this "hellish" doctrine of "no hell" did not stop with Russell and Rutherford is amply made clear in later Witness writings:

It is so plain that the Bible Hell is the tomb, the grave, that even an honest little child can understand it, but not the religious theologians.[40] . . . And now who is responsible for this God-dishonoring doctrine, and what is his purpose? The promulgator of it is Satan Himself; and his purpose in introducing it has been to frighten the people away from studying the Bible and to make them hate God.[41] . . . The doctrine of a burning hell where the wicked are tortured eternally after death cannot be true.[42]

And in an issue of a national magazine, a Jehovah's Witness spokesman answers the question "What Do the Witnesses Believe About Hell?" by saying:

Hell is the grave; it is *not* a place of fiery, eternal torment. Hell is a place of rest, in hope of resurrection, not a place of torture from which one can never escape. Death and hell will both be destroyed at the end of the thousand-year rule of Christ.[43]

What, then, happens to the wicked when they die? They are "destroyed." But at the second advent of Christ, say the Jehovah's Witnesses, all the dead will be raised again and given a second chance to obey God. If they persist in their wickedness and rebellion, they will not suffer eternal torment in some hell; they will be annihilated—this is the second death.

And what do the Jehovah's Witnesses do with Jesus' example of Lazarus and Dives? They ridicule it and evade it and try to explain it away, as they do every other scripture that does not fit in with their delusions. Jehovah's Witnesses claim that the "parable" portrays a coming event which was fulfilled in A.D. 1918. The rich man represents the clergy and Lazarus the "faithful body of Christ." The clergy is constantly tormented by the truth proclaimed through the faithful remnant.[44]

In a recent book, heartily recommended by the Witnesses, is this further explanation of what happens to the dead who died in their sins:

> During the thousand year reign of Christ all the dead shall be awakened and given a fair and impartial trial for life or death; and under that reign the willfully disobedient shall be everlastingly destroyed, while those obedient to the righteous rule of Christ shall be fully restored to human perfection of body, mind, and character. During this millennial reign the earth shall be brought to a state of Edenic paradise and made fit as a place of habitation for perfect man; and man, fully restored to perfection, will inhabit the earth forever.[45]

AND WHAT ABOUT THE FUTURE OF THOSE WHO ARE JEHOVAH'S WITNESSES?

Will they all go to heaven? No, say the Witnesses. Only the "Worthies" of ancient times and those who "inherit the Kingdom of God" will be with Christ in heaven. And, the Witnesses believe, that number is limited to exactly 144,000, and they, with Christ, will be invisible and immortal. What then happens to all others who have lived good lives in obedience to the will of God? The Witnesses explain this as follows:

After mentioning the 144,000 who will go to heaven, Rev. 7 tells of "A great multitude, which no man could number, of all nations," standing before the throne. These are destined to live forever on the earth.[46]

A capsule statement of the Witnesses' faith is given by Milton G. Henschel, director of the Watchtower Bible and Tract Society:

Jehovah will not tolerate wickedness on earth forever. challenged by Satan who caused the rebellion in Eden and who puts the integrity of all men to the test. God's primary purpose is the vindication of this supremacy. In carrying out this purpose, God sent Jesus to earth to provide the ransom sacrifice and to lay the foundation for God's new system of things.

Jehovah will not tolerate wickedness on earth forever. The beginning of the end for Satan came when Christ took power in heaven as King. This happened in 1914. Christ's first act was casting Satan out of heaven, and this was followed by great troubles on earth. This will be climaxed in God's battle, Armageddon: the complete destruction of the Devil and his system of things, his world.[47]

And in answer to the question, "Do Jehovah's Witnesses believe theirs is the only true faith?" Mr. Henschel, in defiant dogmatism, said:

Certainly, if they thought someone else had the true faith, they would preach that.[48]

ARE JEHOVAH'S WITNESSES CHRISTIANS?

Can one be a Christian who denies the deity of Jesus Christ? . . . Who denies the redemptive power of the blood of Christ? . . . Who denies the physical resurrection of Christ? . . . Who denies the bodily return of Christ? . . . Who denies the reality of the Holy Spirit as a Person? . . . Who denies the doctrine of the Trinity and calls it of the devil? . . . Who denies the adequacy of the Bible and, instead of believing the Bible, seeks to *change* it? . . . Who denies that salvation is by faith in Jesus Christ and instead believes that salvation is by works? . . . Who

denies that death is the end of man's probationary period?
. . . Who denies the plain scriptural teaching of the existence of hell? . . . Who denies that the righteous and the
wicked live forever either in heaven or in hell? . . . Who
denies the right to heaven to anyone but Jehovah's Witnesses?

Can anyone who denies so much, and believes so
little of the plain, clear, and unequivocal teaching of the
Bible, be Christian? Please allow John, the apostle of
Christian love, to answer that question:

*Who is a liar but he that denieth that Jesus is the
Christ?* (I John 2:22), and,

*Every spirit that confesseth not that Jesus Christ is
come in the flesh is not of God: and this is that spirit of
antichrist* (I John 4:3).

In the light of John's statement, one must in honesty
and kindness conclude that Jehovah's Witnesses, instead
of being Christians, are victims of one of the most vicious
satanic delusions ever to divert the minds and souls of
men from the true and living God.

WHAT CAN BE SAID IN FAVOR OF JEHOVAH'S WITNESSES?

One can admire their zeal. Whatever else a Jehovah's Witness is, he is zealous. That zeal has made it
possible for the Witnesses to literally girdle the globe with
their teachings, and make converts at the rate of one
thousand a week, and organize one new congregation
somewhere in the world every day in the year.[49]

That zeal has paid off with over 600,000 members, or
"publishers," around the world with approximately 200,-
000 in the United States alone. That zeal has made it
possible for the Witnesses to have unparalleled growth
as represented by the following: During the decade 1942-
52, the number of Jehovah's Witnesses doubled in North
America, multiplied five times in Asia, more than six
times in the Pacific Islands, about seven times in Europe

and Africa, more than twelve times in the Atlantic Islands, and nearly fifteen times in South America[50]—until now the Witnesses have branch offices in 66 countries and work is reported in 159 lands throughout the world.[51]

While 254 other denominations in the United States have registered a 74 per cent increase in their combined membership during the past quarter-century, the Witnesses have leaped ahead with a gain of 2,300 per cent, or at a pace thirty-one times as brisk as all the rest put together.[52]

One can admire their dedication. All of the Witnesses are "ministers," and most of them devote an average of 15 hours a month in Kingdom preaching work. Pioneers are required to give at least 100 hours per month; Special Pioneers and missionaries devote a minimum of 140 hours per month and are sent out to isolated areas and foreign lands where new congregations can be formed. All Pioneers provide for their own support, but the society gives a small allowance to the Special Pioneers in view of their special needs.[53]

Every week, in New York City alone, 7,389 Witnesses put in a total of 26,000 hours of canvassing the 2½ million dwelling units in the 5 boroughs, and have a plan that enables them to cover the entire city three times a year.[54]

The headquarters staff, including the president of the society, Mr. Knorr, are housed in the Bethel Home in Brooklyn (which was built on the site of Henry Ward Beecher's home), and they engage primarily in editorial and printing work, and receive an allowance of fourteen dollars a month in addition to room and board.[55]

These workers printed in 1955 a total of 66,000,000 copies of the *Watchtower* and *Awake,* and also printed over 46,000,000 Bibles, books, and booklets plus 160,000,-000 tracts, calendars, and leaflets. Every day fifteen tons of literature, in sixty-five languages and Braille, rolls off their presses. And the circulation of *Watchtower* is now 2,100,000 copies in forty languages every two weeks, and *Awake* has a circulation of 1,400,000 in thirteen languages every two weeks.[56]

These publications are distributed and sold by the Witnesses with unflagging devotion and earnestness, until one of the more familiar sights of the American landscape is that of Jehovah's Witnesses standing on street corners peddling their magazines and booklets. This, in itself, is sufficient substantiation for Horton Davies characterization of the Jehovah's Witnesses as "a group of religious commercial travellers." [57]

One can admire their familiarity with the Bible. Even though the Witnesses are guilty of wresting the Scriptures to their own destruction, they at least read, and memorize, their Bibles. And in this regard the Witnesses put to shame most of those evangelical Christians who have a high regard for the Bible, but who are woefully lacking in their knowledge of it, and their working familiarity with it.

Why, then, am I a Nazarene and not a Jehovah's Witness?

1. I am not a Jehovah's Witness because, as a Nazarene, I believe that Jesus was more than man—that He was God-Man—

For in him dwelleth all the fulness of the Godhead bodily (Col. 2:9),

and so I could never believe in the Jehovah's Witness Christ, who is nothing more than a man, a good man, even a perfect man, but only a "messenger" from God, who as a mere man "represented" God on earth for a few short years.

2. I am not a Jehovah's Witness because, as a Nazarene, I believe in the redemptive power of the blood of Christ—

In whom we have redemption through his blood, the forgiveness of sins, according to the riches of his grace (Eph. 1:7),

and so I could never believe in the Jehovah's Witness Christ, who, as a man, died only to provide a "ransom" and whose death meant only that a lonely man was dying on a meaningless cross.

3. I am not a Jehovah's Witness because, as a Nazarene, I believe in the Christ who physically rose from the grave—

And declared to be the Son of God with power, according to the spirit of holiness, by the resurrection from the dead (Rom. 1:4),

and so I never could believe in the Jehovah's Witness Christ, who is "dead, forever dead."

4. I am not a Jehovah's Witness because, as a Nazarene, I believe in the Christ who is coming back to earth again even in like manner as He went away—

Which also said, Ye men of Galilee, why stand ye gazing up into heaven? this same Jesus, which is taken up from you into heaven, shall so come in like manner as ye have seen him go into heaven (Acts 1:11),

and so I could never believe in the Jehovah's Witness Christ, who came back to earth in 1914 and is now invisible, only waiting for the Battle of Armageddon, when He will avenge himself of His enemies.

5. I am not a Jehovah's Witness because, as a Nazarene, I believe the Bible to be the inspired Word of God—

All scripture is given by inspiration of God, and is profitable for doctrine, for reproof, for correction, for instruction in righteousness (II Tim. 3:16), and so I could never believe the Jehovah's Witness perversions of the Bible or that the Bible had to be "Russellized" before it could be meaningful to those in search of truth.

6. I am not a Jehovah's Witness because, as a Nazarene, I believe in the reality of the Holy Spirit as a Person—

Howbeit when he, the Spirit of truth, is come, he will guide you into all truth: for he shall not speak of himself; but whatsoever he shall hear, that shall he speak: and he will shew you things to come (John 16:13),

and so I could never believe in the Jehovah's Witness "Spirit," who is "not God," but only the "influence" of Jehovah.

7. I am not a Jehovah's Witness because, as a Nazarene, I believe that death is the end of man's probationary period—

It is appointed unto men once to die, but after this the judgment (Heb. 9:27),

and so I could never believe the Jehovah's Witness heresy that death is extinction, annihilation, and that during the millennium all will be raised again for a second chance at salvation.

8. I am not a Jehovah's Witness because, as a Nazarene, I believe that salvation comes only through faith in the atoning blood of Christ—

Not by works of righteousness which we have done, but according to his mercy he saved us, by the washing of regeneration, and renewing of the Holy Ghost; which he shed on us abundantly through Jesus Christ our Saviour (Titus 3:5-6),

and so I could never believe in the Jehovah's Witness "salvation" by works—regardless of how frantic or how sacrificial.

9. I am not a Jehovah's Witness because, as a Nazarene, I believe in a future life of eternal reward, or punishment, for everyone—

And these shall go away into everlasting punishment: but the righteous into life eternal (Matt. 25:46),

and so I could never believe the Jehovah's Witness lie that hell is nonexistent and that the wicked will be annihilated while heaven will be reserved only for those choice "Witnesses," 144,000, while all the rest of those who have been obedient to God during their lives will be relegated to this earth, where they will eat, drink, propagate, and live forever with perfect mortal bodies in an Edenic paradise.

10. I am not a Jehovah's Witness because, as a Nazarene, I believe that no man as questionable in morals, disreputable in character, and distorted in thinking as Charles Taze Russell could be the founder of a religion that is the only true revelation of God, the only remedy for the ills and injustices of this world, and the only hope for the life to come.

The world is becoming full of impostors—men who will not admit that Jesus the Christ really became man. Now this is the very spirit of deceit and is anti-christ. . . . The man who is so "advanced" that he is not content with what Christ taught, has in fact no God. . . .

If any teacher comes to you who is disloyal to what Christ taught, don't have him inside your house. Don't even wish him "God-speed," unless you want to share in the evil that he is doing.

—II John 1:7, 9-10 (Phillips)

Chapter Five

WHY I AM A NAZARENE

and Not a Christian Scientist

WHAT IS A CHRISTIAN SCIENTIST?

In answering this question George Channing, internationally known Christian Science lecturer and practitioner, says: "A Christian Scientist is one who accepts and practices Christian Science as his religion."[1]

WHO IS THE FOUNDER OF CHRISTIAN SCIENCE?

According to Christian Scientists, Mary Baker Eddy was the discoverer and founder of Christian Science and the revelator of truth to this age. While it is true that Mrs. Eddy founded the Christian Science church, the ideas and methods of healing which form the basis of Christian Science were taken, appropriated, and stolen directly from a healer in Maine by the name of Phineas P. Quimby. So while Mary Baker Eddy was the founder and "mother" of the church, Phineas P. Quimby was the "father" of its system of ideas and healing practices.

Before Mrs. Eddy's debt to Mr. Quimby can be understood, however, it is necessary to know something of the early years of Mary Baker, and the forces that shaped her life and that helped her to become Mary Baker Glover Patterson Eddy, high priestess and prophetess and "Mother Mary" to almost a million susceptible souls called "Christian Scientists."

Mary Baker was born July 16, 1821, in the New Hampshire town of Bow, located about five miles north of Concord. She was the sixth child born to Mark and Abigail Baker, industrious farmers and respected members of the Congregational church. Mary was a highly sensitive child, who very early manifested the signs of serious nervous disorders that were to plague her all through life. When she was only eight she began to hear voices calling her name, and when her mother became alarmed about it she suggested that Mary should not be allowed to read and study so much. Her father readily agreed, saying, "Take the books away from her; her brain is too big for her body."

Being tutored at home, young Mary Baker soon found that, because she was sensitive and highly nervous, her parents indulged her whims, and when crossed, she could get her way by having a nervous "spell," falling upon the floor and lying there rigid until her parents gave in. Even as an adult Mary never really outgrew these temper tantrums.

When Mary was fifteen she moved with her family to a farm near Tilton, New Hampshire, where she enrolled in the Tilton Academy. It was here, in her parents' home, in December of 1843, that she married George Washington Glover, a building contractor from Charleston, South Carolina. A few months following the wedding, young George Glover died of yellow fever, and the young wife, grief-stricken, but with considerable cash from the liquidation of her husband's business, went back to her parents' home in New England, where in September she gave birth to a son, whom she named after her late husband.

Because of Mary's extreme nervousness she was never able to take care of her own son and a neighbor was hired to look after him. When the neighbor married and moved to another town, it was thought best to let the son go with the neighbor, and so Mary never was able to rear her own son. Instead she was treated as an invalid in the home of her parents, as her health seemed to be completely broken. A psychiatrist could possibly explain Mary's peculiar passion at this time for being rocked. And to satisfy her whim her father would take her on his lap and rock her. Her father even put rockers on Mary's bed, tied a rope to it, led the rope through the window, and had the hired man pull the rope gently to keep the bed rocking, which seemed to soothe her troubled spirits.

In 1853, at thirty-two years of age and in ill health, Mary Baker Glover met and married a traveling dentist by the name of Dr. Daniel Patterson. Mary was so frail and weak at the time of her wedding that her husband had to carry her downstairs from her room for the ceremony and then carry her back to her room on its completion. After several years of being subjected to the neurotic whims of his exacting and invalid wife, Dr. Patterson deserted her for another woman, after which Mary divorced him in Salem, Massachusetts.

Strangely enough, it is to Dr. Patterson that Mary was indebted for first hearing about the man who was to change her life—and the lives of thousands who call themselves Christian Scientists. For it was Dr. Patterson who first told Mary of the strange little healer in Portland, Maine, by the name of "Dr." Phineas P. Quimby. It was Dr. Patterson, in fact, who wrote Quimby to see if he would come and heal his frail and enfeebled wife. Quimby replied that he could not leave Portland, but that if Mrs. Patterson would come to Portland he was sure that he could heal her.

So in October of 1862, Mary Baker Patterson arrived in Portland, Maine, and immediately went to see "Dr." Quimby. After listening to her story, Quimby told her that she was not sick at all—that her animal spirit was reflecting its grief upon her body, and the doctors were calling it spinal disease. So after wetting his hands in a basin of water, Quimby began to massage her head to impart what he called "healthy electricity," and before long had her in a state of hypnosis from which she awoke freed of her pain.

Mary's enthusiasm for Quimby's healing art and method knew no bounds, and before she left Portland she wrote a glowing account of her healing for a Portland newspaper and even dramatized Quimby's healing powers by climbing the 182 steps to the dome of the City Hall.

After a short while, however, Mary felt herself slipping back into her state of nervous illness and so decided to make another trip to see Quimby. On this second visit she sought to learn the secret of Quimby's healing method and in long conversations with him tried to convince him that he was accomplishing his healings through the method Christ used, but Quimby could see no relationship between his mesmerism and spiritual, or Christian, principles.

In fact Quimby was very frank in stating the secret of his healings. "My practice," he said, "is unlike all medical practice. I give no medicine, and make no outward applications. I tell the patient his troubles, and what he thinks is his disease, and my explanation is the cure. If I succeed in correcting his errors, I change the fluids of the system, and establish the patient in health. The truth is the cure."[2] Some of Quimby's manuscripts, which have since been published, reveal that he referred to his new mind-healing system as "Christian Science," and that he called disease "an error," and that "disease is false reasoning. False reasoning is sickness and death."[3]

So this erstwhile clock repairman, this self-styled "Dr." who had never studied medicine, but who had stumbled into the principles of mesmerism and hypnosis and psychic suggestion, gave to Mrs. Mary Baker Patterson the basic principles of a system of healing that she was to overlay and elaborate with her own weird theories of Christian "truth" until the world would know the whole system as "Christian Science" and hundreds of thousands would respect it as an "inspired" religion.

Significantly enough, it was not until the year 1866, when "Dr." Quimby died of an ulcer, that Mary Baker Patterson claimed to be the founder of "Christian Science." It was only then, of course, that Mary felt safe in claiming authorship to Quimby's ideas, since Quimby was no longer around to dispute that claim.

One evening in that year of 1866, Mrs. Patterson slipped and fell on the ice and was picked up unconscious, and when the doctor examined her he said that her injuries were of an internal nature and described her condition as critical. In a few days, when she and others thought that she was dying, Mary opened her Bible and read the story of Jesus' healing the man sick of the palsy. And when she read the words, "Thy faith hath saved thee," it seemed that those words were the catalyst combining all of Quimby's ideas and her own fanciful thoughts into one great and fundamental Christian "truth." She immediately got up from the bed and walked about and from that moment was obsessed with the thought of teaching others this great healing principle of "Christian Science."

Mrs. Patterson soon rented some second-story rooms of a house in Lynn, Massachusetts, and opened her school, calling it "The Metaphysical College." The instruction in this "College" was rather expensive—$300 for a series of twelve half-hour lectures, which were later reduced to seven lectures—with no reduction in cost.

In 1875, at the age of fifty-four, Mary Baker Patterson published her first edition of *Science and Health with Key to the Scriptures*. Two years later she married a bachelor by the name of Asa Gilbert Eddy, a salesman for a sewing machine company. With at last a published product to sell, and a good salesman to sell it, business picked up. And with the book selling for $3.00 a copy, money began coming in in ever increasing amounts. This enabled Mary to organize, in 1892, the "Mother Church," and to start publication of the *Christian Science Journal,* the official organ of her organization. In 1894, the First Church of Christ, Scientist, costing a quarter of a million dollars, was dedicated in Boston.

Whether Christian Science has been profitable to the cause of Christianity or to the world is debatable, but there is no doubt whatsoever that it was profitable to Mary Baker Eddy, for with her income from the church and her publications—*Science and Health,* and *Sentinel,* and the world-famous newspaper, the *Christian Science Monitor,* along with her other writings—she was able to accumulate a fortune conservatively estimated at two million dollars by the time she died, December 3, 1910, at the age of eighty-nine.

WHAT IS CHRISTIAN SCIENCE?

It is a system of beliefs about mind and matter with particular reference to healing. As Mr. Channing says:

> Christian science is the belief that God is divine Mind, the conceiver of man and the universe, and Mind is all that exists. Spirit is eternal and real; matter is an unreal illusion subject to decay and dissolution. Evil has to do with matter—therefore evil is unreal, an illusion. Death is an illusion of the mortal sense. Man, the idea and image of God, is immortal, perfect, wholly good, untouched and untainted by evil because man expresses God. Disease and illness are aspects of falsehood—delusions of the human mind which can be destroyed by the prayer of spiritual understanding.[4]

It is actually incredible that almost a million people really *believe* such fantastic falsehoods. In a world where hospitals are filled with sick and crushed and diseased bodies, how can anyone actually believe that "disease and illness are delusions of the human mind"?

In a world of base and black and wretched sin, how can anyone actually believe that "evil is unreal, an illusion"?

In a world of slave-labor camps and extermination ovens and human degeneracies and debaucheries and brutal butcheries, how can anyone actually believe that "man is perfect, wholly good, untouched and untainted by evil"?

How can anyone, in a world whose surface is gashed with graves, in a world where everyone must someday stand and look at eyes that will never see again, and lips that will never kiss again, and hands that will never clasp again—how can anyone then walk away from that cold casket and actually believe that "death is an illusion of mortal sense"?

No, Mr. Quimby and Mrs. Eddy and Mr. Channing, even if the Bible were a forgery and Christ were a counterfeit, no one who had ever really faced up to life could ever believe in Christian Science.

I. What Do Christian Scientists Believe About Jesus Christ?

They deny His deity. Mrs. Eddy declares:

> Jesus Christ is not God, as Jesus himself declared, but is the Son of God. This declaration, understood, conflicts not at all with another of his sayings: "I and my Father are one,"—that is, one in quality, not in quantity. As a drop of water is one with the ocean, a ray of light one with the sun, even so God and man, Father and son, are one in being.[5]

Instead of accepting the scriptural account of Jesus' birth as found in Luke 2:26-35, Mrs. Eddy presents her own idea:

> The Virgin-Mother conceived this idea of God, and gave to her ideal the name of Jesus—that is, Joshua, or Savior. The illumination of Mary's spiritual sense put to silence material law and its order of generation, and brought forth her child by the revelation of Truth, demonstrating God as the Father of men. The Holy Ghost, or divine Spirit, overshadowed the pure sense of the Virgin-Mother with the full recognition that being is Spirit.

> The Christ dwelt forever an idea in the bosom of God, the
> divine Principle of the man Jesus, and woman perceived this
> spiritual idea, though at first faintly developed.[6]

Is there anyone who actually believes that this is a
superior explanation to that given in Luke?

THEY DENY CHRIST'S SECOND COMING

Christian Scientists reject the simple statement of
scripture that "this same Jesus . . . shall so come in like
manner as ye have seen him go into heaven," and accept, rather, the fanstastic assertion of Mrs. Eddy that
"the second appearance of Jesus is unquestionably the
spiritual advent of the advancing idea of God in Christian
Science."[7]

How can those, then, who deny the deity of Jesus
Christ, who deny the redemptive meaning of the birth,
death, and resurrection of Christ, and who deny the
second coming of Christ—how can such men and women,
with any candor at all, claim to be "Christian" Scientists?

II. WHAT DO CHRISTIAN SCIENTISTS BELIEVE ABOUT THE BIBLE?

Like other cultists, Christian Scientists profess great
respect for the Bible—and then set about to deny its
clear teachings and pervert its saving gospel. Mrs. Eddy
insisted that the source of her doctrine was sacred scripture, but as Dr. Mayer says, "The fact is that Mrs. Eddy
considered the Bible a dark book which could not be
understood without the 'key of David' which key she, of
course, supplied."

Dr. Mayer continues:

> By no stretch of the imagination can the Christian
> Scientists claim the Bible as the source of their theology.
> In reality Mrs. Eddy's *Science and Health* is the source
> of religious truths in the Christian Science Church. She
> maintained that while the Bible is full of mistakes, her book
> contains the real, unadulterated truth; that it is the perfect
> word of God inspired without error by the Holy Ghost.[8]

As a noted Christian Science writer said:

Christian Scientists feel that Mrs. Eddy's book, *Science and Health with Key to the Scriptures,* offers the complete spiritual meaning of the Bible. They believe that this full meaning would not have been available to them without Mrs. Eddy's discovery.[9]

Mrs. Eddy, of course, went beyond this evaluation and boldly claimed that her book was *inspired:*

I should blush to write of *Science and Health with Key to the Scriptures* as I have, were it of human origin, and I, apart from God, its author; but as I was only a scribe echoing the harmonies of heaven in divine metaphysics, I cannot be super-modest in my estimate of the Christian Science textbook.[10]

But it was not only the "textbook" that was "inspired"—*all* her writings on Christian Science were "inspired of God." And if anyone doubts that, all that is necessary to clarify the matter is to ask Mrs. Eddy and she answers:

The works that I have written on Christian Science contain absolute Truth. I was a scribe under orders, and who can refrain from transcribing what God indites?[11]

Here, again, is the cultist's approach: "Yes, we believe the Bible, but this book of ours will explain the Bible and, in many cases, say it better." It is impossible to estimate the damage that has been done by these people who come saying, "The Bible—*and* our book."

III. WHAT DO CHRISTIAN SCIENTISTS BELIEVE ABOUT SALVATION?

When one learns that Christian Scientists deny the deity of Jesus Christ and refuse to accept the Bible as meaningful and valid until it has been "Eddyized," it is not exactly startling to learn that their beliefs concerning salvation are some of the most twisted and distorted that Satan ever suggested to deluded minds.

Before one can get a clear picture of their distortions concerning salvation, however, one must understand something of what Christian Scientists believe about sin.

The following "explanation" of the doctrine of sin is as good an example as any of the mumbo jumbo which is Christian Science:

> Man is really sinless and free. Sin is the belief in the real existence of a mind or minds other than the divine mind, God. Mortal mind, which believes in decaying and dying, is the sinner. St. Paul called it the "carnal" mind. If a person accepts the carnal mind, its sins will appear to be his sins, its suffering his suffering. Christian Scientists rid themselves of sin by breaking the false notion that the carnal mind is real, or one's own. Penalty for sin lasts only as long as such false belief lasts.
>
> Christian Scientists hold that sin is unreal. But this does not mean that one can sin with impunity. The sinner does not know that sin is unreal; if he did, this would destroy his capacity for sinning.[12]

Does anyone actually believe that? Indeed. It is an official pronouncement approved by the Mother Church, and believed by every true Christian Scientist.

With such distorted ideas of sin—ideas that essentially deny sin—where, and to whom, would one look for salvation? Mrs. Eddy answers it this way:

> The destruction of sin is the divine method of pardon. Divine Life destroys death, Truth destroys error, and Love destroys hate. Being destroyed, sin needs no other form of forgiveness.[13]

Mrs. Eddy not only rejects Christ as the only Saviour; she ridicules the whole orthodox Christian concept of salvation when she says:

> Does erudite theology regard the crucifixion of Jesus chiefly as providing a ready pardon for all sinners who ask for it and are willing to be forgiven? Then we must differ from them . . . The efficacy of the crucifixion lay in the practical affection and goodness it demonstrated for mankind . . . One sacrifice, however great, is insufficient to pay the debt of sin. The atonement requires constant self-immolation on the sinner's part.
>
> The spiritual essence of blood is sacrifice. The efficacy of Jesus' spiritual offering is infinitely greater than can be expressed by our sense of human blood. The ma-

terial blood of Jesus was no more efficacious to cleanse from
sin when it was shed upon "the accursed tree," than when
it was flowing in his veins as he went daily about his
Father's business. His true flesh and blood were his Life;
and they truly eat his flesh and drink his blood, who
partake of that divine Life.[14]

Christ, then, to Christian Scientists is not the Saviour
who "was once offered to bear the sins of many" (Heb.
9: 28). He is only the "Way-Shower," a guide to show
men how they can free themselves from all error by practicing the "truth" of "divine science."

IV. WHAT DO CHRISTIAN SCIENTISTS BELIEVE ABOUT THE FUTURE LIFE?

To Christian Scientists there is neither heaven nor
hell, in a geographical sense, for as Mrs. Eddy said, "The
sinner makes his own hell by doing evil, and the saint his
own heaven by doing right." Both heaven and hell, to a
Christian Scientist, are symbolic of states of mind.[15]

Heaven is not a locality, but a divine state of Mind
in which all the manifestations of Mind are harmonious
and immortal, because sin is not there and man is found
having no righteousness of his own, but in possession of the
"mind of the Lord," as the Scriptures say.[16]

Whatever else may be said of this denial of heaven
as a place, Mrs. Eddy's heaven is not the one Christians
have always believed in and looked forward to because,
as readers of the Bible and lovers of Christ, they have
thrilled to the promise of Jesus when He said: "In my
Father's house are many mansions: if it were not so,
I would have told you. I go to prepare a place for you"
(John 14: 2).

Mrs. Eddy defines hell as:

Mortal belief; error; lust; remorse; hatred; revenge;
sin; sickness; death; suffering and self-destruction; self-
imposed agony; effects of sin; that which "worketh abom-
ination or maketh a lie."[17]

No wonder there are those who find Christian
Science a "comforting" religion, when it helps them to

reject the clear teaching of God's Word that hell is a "place" of "outer darkness," a "furnace of fire," "where their worm dieth not, and the fire is not quenched." But rejecting God's Word is not refuting God's Word.

WHAT DO CHRISTIAN SCIENTISTS BELIEVE ABOUT HEALING?

The most commonly held impression of Christian Science is that it is a system of healing by prayer. Nothing could be further from the truth. Mrs. Eddy consistently and explicitly denied that the healings accomplished by Christian Science were accomplished through prayer. It was the denial of the reality of sickness and pain—the realization that suffering and illness existed only in the mind—that *realization* of the truth was the healing.

Mrs. Eddy wrote, concerning prayer for the sick:

> The common custom of praying for the recovery of the sick finds help in blind belief, whereas help should come from the enlightened understanding. Changes in belief may go on indefinitely, but they are the merchandise of human thought and not the outgrowth of divine science.[18]

In commenting on the healing practices of Christian Science, Dr. Mayer says:

> Strictly speaking, Christian Science does not teach bodily healing from sickness. There is no basis for the idea of suggestion. Mortal mind, according to Eddyism, cannot possibly heal, since it is the Cause of error of disease. The "healing" method of Christian Scientists consists in "demonstrating" the principle that there is no matter; that everything is Divine Mind, which is perfect, sinless, and incapable of sickness or death.[19]

Prayer for the sick, then, as for anything else, would be a sheer waste of time to the Christian Scientist. All that is necessary is to "understand" the Divine Mind, and that *"understanding"* will bring one whatever benefits the "impersonal Principle" called God has to share.

Even the Lord's Prayer has been drained of its great personal implications by Mrs. Eddy's interpretation of it.

This is what she calls "the spiritual sense" of it:

"Our Father which art in heaven,"

Our Father-Mother God, all-harmonious

"Hallowed be thy name."

Adorable One.

"Thy kingdom come."

Thy kingdom is come; Thou art ever ever-present.

"Thy will be done in earth, as it is in heaven."

Enable us to know—as in heaven, so on earth—God is omnipotent, supreme.

"Give us this day our daily bread."

Give us grace for today; feed the famished affections;

"And forgive us our debts, as we forgive our debtors."

And love is reflected in love;

"And lead us not into temptation, but deliver us from evil: "

And God leadeth us not into temptation, but delivereth us from sin, disease, and death.

"For thine is the kingdom, and the power, and the glory for ever."

For God is infinite, all-power, all-life, truth, love, over all, and all.[20]

There are many reported healings attributed to Christian Science, but not one of them is achieved by what the Christian understands as prayer. In fact, 100 pages in Mrs. Eddy's *Science and Health with Key to the Scriptures* is given to the testimonials of those who have been healed by Christian Science. And to read those testimonials in *Science and Health* and those in every issue of the *Christian Science Journal* and each weekly issue of the *Sentinel,* one cannot help but think of the glowing testimonials published by the promoters of every cure-all patent medicine that was ever sold to a gullible public. In fact, one is almost brought to the conclusion that Christian Science, in its healing claims, is little more than "mental Hadacol."

WHAT DO CHRISTIAN SCIENTISTS BELIEVE ABOUT THE HOLY SPIRIT?

To the Christian Scientist, the Holy Spirit is nothing more than Christian Science; and to receive the Holy Spirit, to a Christian Scientist, means nothing more or less than to come to a deeper understanding of the teachings of Mary Baker Eddy. Does that statement seem exaggerated? Listen to Mrs. Eddy's own explanation:

> In the words of St. John: "He shall give you another Comforter, that He may be with you forever." This Comforter I understand to be Divine Science.[21]

And how does Mrs. Eddy explain the coming of the Holy Spirit on the Day of Pentecost?

> His [Jesus'] students then received the Holy Ghost. By this is meant, that by all they had witnessed and suffered, they were roused to an enlarged understanding of divine Science, even to the spiritual interpretation and discernment of Jesus's teachings and demonstrations, which gave them a faint conception of the Life which is God. They no longer measured man by material sense. After gaining the true idea of their glorified Master, they became better healers, leaning no longer on matter, but on the divine Principle of their work. The influx of light was sudden. It was sometimes an overwhelming power as on the Day of Pentecost.[22]

And if one is still in doubt that Mrs. Eddy equates Christian Science with the Holy Ghost, these words should settle the matter completely:

> The theory of three persons in one God (that is, a personal trinity or Tri-unity) suggests polytheism rather than the one ever-present I AM. . . . Life, Truth, and Love constitute the triune Person called God,—that is, the triply divine Principle, Love. They represent a trinity in unity, three in one,—the same essence, though multiform in office: God the Father-Mother; Christ the spiritual idea of sonship; divine Science or the Holy Comforter. These three express in divine Science the threefold, essential nature of the infinite.[23]

There, in concentrated form, is the reservoir of religious blasphemy from which have flowed ever widening streams of polluted doctrines and perverted theories which have poisoned the minds and souls of countless thousands of men and women who have called themselves Christian Scientists.

Christian Science is seen, then, as neither Christian nor scientific. How can any system be Christian when it denies every major tenet of the orthodox Christian faith: the personality of God . . . the deity of Christ . . . the reality of the Holy Spirit as a Person . . . the efficacy of the blood of Christ . . . the redemptive meaning of the resurrection, ascension, and second coming of Christ . . . the fact of sin, sickness, and death . . . the clear, scriptural teaching of the judgment, and heaven and hell?

How can any system be scientific when it is based on the aberrations of a clockmaker turned quack and overlayed with the religious fantasies of a neurotic woman who dabbled in metaphysics? The whole system must in fairness and honesty be judged unchristian and unscientific.

WHAT ATTITUDE SHOULD CHRISTIANS HAVE TOWARD CHRISTIAN SCIENTISTS?

A Christian must totally reject the whole distorted system called Christian Science but, at the same time, have Christian love and charity toward every Christian Scientist. Christians are not against *persons;* Christians are against wrong *principles.*

All Christians can admire the quiet but dedicated zeal of those who profess to believe in Christian Science —a zeal and dedication that in no sense approaches the frenzied intensity of, say, a Jehovah's Witness, but a more sophisticated zeal that finds its greatest effectiveness with the upper and middle classes of society.

This sophisticated sharing of an idea has resulted in a religious organization with over 3,000 churches,[24] most of which are well located in the larger cities, and each of which must be paid for before it is dedicated. It is impossible to get official statistics as to the number of Christian Scientists, as Mrs. Eddy forbade the publishing of membership figures in any Church of Christ, Scientist. Informed estimates, however, range from 275,000 to 400,000, but as Frank S. Mead points out, "The number of people studying Christian Science and attending its services but not yet admitted to full membership exceeds the number who have been so admitted."[25]

Why, then, am I not a Christian Scientist?

1. I am not a Christian Scientist because, as a Nazarene, I believe that God is a Person—

Unto thee it was shewed, that thou mightest know that the Lord he is God; there is none else beside him (Deut. 4:35),

and so I could never believe in the Christian Scientist's God, who is quite largely an "impersonal principle."

2. I am not a Christian Scientist because, as a Nazarene, I believe in the Christ who is God's Son, who died, arose, ascended, and is coming back to earth again "even as he went away"—

Concerning his Son Jesus Christ our Lord, which was made of the seed of David according to the flesh; and declared to be the Son of God with power, according to the spirit of holiness, by the resurrection from the dead (Rom. 1:3-4),

and so I could never believe in the Christ of the Christian Scientist, who was nothing more than an "idea," and exists only as an influence in furthering "divine Science."

3. I am not a Christian Scientist because, as a Nazarene, I believe in the reality of sin—

Whosoever committeth sin transgresseth also the law: for sin is the transgression of the law (I John 3:4); and,

If we say that we have not sinned, we make him a liar, and his word is not in us (I John 1:10),

and so I could never believe the Christian Scientist lie that "sin is unreal, an illusion of material sense."

4. I am not a Christian Scientist because, as a Nazarene, I believe in the forgiving and cleansing power of the blood of Christ—

Forasmuch as ye know that ye were not redeemed with corruptible things, as silver and gold, from your vain conversation received by tradition from your fathers; but with the precious blood of Christ, as of a lamb without blemish and without spot (I Pet. 1:18-19),

and so I could never believe the Christian Scientist's heresy that the blood of Jesus "was no more efficacious to cleanse from sin when it was shed upon 'the accursed tree' than when it was flowing in his veins as he went daily about his Father's business."

5. I am not a Christian Scientist because, as a Nazarene, I believe in the reality of the Holy Spirit as a Person—

But the Comforter, which is the Holy Ghost, whom the Father will send in my name, he shall teach you all things, and bring all things to your remembrance, whatsoever I have said unto you (John 14:26),

and so I could never believe in the Christian Science blasphemy that "the Holy Ghost is Christian Science."

6. I am not a Christian Scientist because, as a Nazarene, I believe the Bible is the Word of God with no needed additions or subtractions—

But these are written, that ye might believe that Jesus is the Christ, the Son of God; and that believing ye might have life through his name (John 20:31),

and so I could never believe the Christian Scientist's dictum that the Bible must be "Eddyized" before it can be meaningful and valid.

7. I am not a Christian Scientist because, as a Nazarene, I believe the scriptural teaching on the judgment and on heaven and hell—

And many of them that sleep in the dust of the earth shall awake, some to everlasting life, and some to shame and everlasting contempt (Dan. 12:2),

and so I could never believe in the Christian Science "heaven" and "hell" as merely states of mind.

8. I am not a Christian Scientist because, as a Nazarene, I believe that divine healing comes in response to prayer and faith—

Is any sick among you? let him call for the elders of the church; and let them pray over him, anointing him with oil in the name of the Lord: and the prayer of faith shall save the sick, and the Lord shall raise him up; and if he have committed sins, they shall be forgiven him (Jas. 5:14-15),

and so I could never believe the Christian Scientist idea that the way to be healed of sickness and disease is to merely deny their existence as "errors of the mortal mind."

9. I am not a Christian Scientist because, as a Nazarene, I believe that a religion that is spiritually valid would have to be founded on something more substantial than an unbelieving quack and a neurotic heretic—

For other foundation can no man lay than that is laid, which is Jesus Christ (I Cor. 3:11).

10. I am not a Christian Scientist because, as a Nazarene, I believe in the faith "once delivered unto the saints"—

Beloved, when I gave all diligence to write unto you of the common salvation, it was needful for me to write unto you, and exhort you that ye should earnestly contend for the faith which was once delivered unto the saints (Jude 3),

and so I could never believe in a religious system that is a denial of everything Christian and a perversion of everything scientific.

Beware of anyone getting hold of you by means of a theosophy which is specious make-believe, on the lines of human tradition, corresponding to the elemental spirits of the world and not to Christ.

—Col. 2:8 (Moffatt)

Chapter Six

WHY I AM A NAZARENE

and Not a Seventh-Day Adventist

WHAT IS A SEVENTH-DAY ADVENTIST?

Although it is impossible to answer this question briefly, it can be said that a Seventh-Day Adventist is one who believes in the soon personal return or advent of Christ to this earth and believes, unlike other adventists and other Christians, that one cannot be a true Christian unless the Sabbath is observed on the seventh day of the week, or Saturday, instead of the first day, or Sunday.

WHO WAS THE FOUNDER OF SEVENTH-DAY ADVENTISM?

The founder of the Seventh-Day Adventist church was a woman by the name of Ellen Harmon White. As the name Mary Baker Eddy is identified with Christian Science, so the name Ellen Harmon White is identified with Seventh-Day Adventism. These two religious movements have at least one thing in common in that both were founded by visionary, neurotic women.

Ellen Harmon was born at Gorham, Maine, November 26, 1827. While she was still a child her family moved to Portland, Maine, where, when only nine years of age, she suffered an accident which was to have unusual influence in her life. A playmate struck her with a stone and knocked little Ellen unconscious, and she remained in that state for three weeks. Her face was disfigured and her nervous system suffered a great shock. Her health, in fact, became so poor that she had to give up school, and with the exception of a short period of tutoring at home she received no further formal education.

When Ellen Harmon was only seventeen years of age she began to have those "visions" that were later to be called "inspired," and these visions were to form the basis of the strange and distorted doctrines of the Seventh-Day Adventists.

There would never have been a Seventh-Day Adventist church, however, if it had not been for a one-time Baptist minister by the name of William Miller. Miller was born at Pittsfield, Massachusetts, in 1782. Even though a busy farmer-preacher, he devoted a great amount of time to reading his Bible, and in 1831 announced that he had discovered the exact date when Christ would return to earth. He based his calculations on the 2,300 years of Dan. 8:14, and so, according to Miller, Christ's second advent would occur October 22, 1843.

The announcement of that date created tremendous excitement and there were those who gave away their property and left their crops to rot in the fields and on the great day—October 22, 1843—they put on their white ascension robes and waited for the moment when Christ would appear. When the day came and nothing happened, Miller announced that he had miscalculated by exactly one year, and said that it was October 22, 1844, that was to be the time of Christ's second advent. Again there was great excitement and preparations were made to be "caught up to meet the Lord in the air." But when that day passed by without the Lord's return, thousands of Millerites (or Adventists) lost all faith in the predictions and drifted into other religious movements of the day, and of course some of them repudiated Adventism all together.

Even William Miller himself, after the two predictions had failed, repudiated his system of prophecy,

and in the following words he humbly and honestly renounced the whole foundation upon which Adventism
rests:

> On the passing of the published time, I frankly ac-
> knowledged my disappointment. We expected the personal
> coming of Christ at that time; and now to contend that we
> were not mistaken is dishonest. We should never be
> ashamed frankly to confess our errors. I have no con-
> fidence in any of the new theories that grew out of that
> movement. . . .[1]

If everyone had been as honest as William Miller,
there would be no Adventist churches today. But not
everyone was that honest and so there were many
fanciful theories which immediately began to sprout from
Miller's discredited Adventism. In fact, there were at
least six divisions of Adventists that resulted from Miller's
unfulfilled prophecies, the most important division being
the Seventh-Day Adventists.[2] And the leader of that
division was Mrs. Ellen Harmon White, who, in 1845,
picked up the pieces of Miller's repudiated theories and
built them into one of the most fantastic systems of belief that ever rested on a delusion.

When William Miller's prophecy failed, Ellen Harmon was deeply disappointed and disturbed. Her health
failed rapidly and she seemed to lose all hope and all
reason for living. In December of 1844, two months after
the failure of Miller's prophecy, Ellen was kneeling in
prayer one day with four other women, and while she
was praying, a "vision" came to her in which she seemed
to be transported to heaven and shown the experiences
that awaited those who would be faithful to the Advent
"gospel."

It was not long, however, before she began having
other visions, accompanied by strange physical manifestations. According to the reports of the doctors and
others, her eyes remained open during these "visions";
she ceased to breathe; and during these trances she per-

formed miraculous feats. The main burden of the "visions" seemed to be the messages she would receive for individuals, families, and churches.

On August 30, 1846, Ellen Harmon married Rev. James White, a preacher of the Advent faith, and together, in 1849, they began publishing a little paper which soon became known as the *Advent Review and Sabbath Herald.* This became the organ of the Advent movement and for years Mr. White was in charge of the publishing interests of the Adventists.

At a conference in Battle Creek, Michigan, in September, 1860, the name "Seventh-Day Adventist" was officially adopted, and in May of 1863 a formal denominational organization was established, with a constituency of 125 churches and 3,500 members.[3]

In 1874, Ellen Harmon White and her husband established the Seventh-Day Adventist magazine *Signs of the Times,* and this magazine became a very useful propaganda tool for the spreading of the ideas and doctrines of Ellen White, which ideas and doctrines were becoming ever more fanciful and Bible-distorting.

After Mr. White died, in 1881, Mrs. White traveled extensively, visiting churches and attending conferences and camp meetings and spreading her peculiar theories about the Sabbath and the second coming of Christ. These travels took her to Europe in 1885, and then in 1891 she went to Australia, where she remained for nine years.

Although Mrs. Ellen White never claimed to be a leader of the church—only a "voice," a "messenger" bearing communications from God to His people (the Seventh-Day Adventists), she played a very important part in most of the early decisions of the denomination: in moving the denominational headquarters to Washington, D.C., and, in 1909, helping to found the College of Medical Evangelists at Loma Linda, California—an institution that has in many ways brought prestige and fame to the Seventh-Day Adventist church.

Mrs. White was a prolific, if fanciful, writer. Her books include: *The Great Controversy Between Christ and Satan; The Desire of Ages; Testimonies for the Church; Prophets and Kings;* and others. And between and during the writing of the books, she was busy writing for all the publications—the papers, the magazines, the leaflets, etc.—that helped spread the cause of Seventh-Day Adventism.

After a long life of hard work, of extensive traveling, of much writing, of founding and helping to develop a new church, Mrs. Ellen White died, at eighty-one, at St. Helena, California, July 16, 1915. But not before she was able to see the Seventh-Day Adventist church—the church of which she was the "founder and Prophetess and Messenger"—established and growing and filling the minds of thousands with some of the weirdest religious fantasies that ever came from the distorted mind of a frail and neurotic woman.[4]

Just as Brigham Young took the strange, sensual revelations of Joseph Smith and built the Mormon church; and Judge Rutherford took the weird distortions of Charles Taze Russell and built the human conglomeration known as Jehovah's Witnesses; and as Mary Baker Eddy took the healing quackeries of Phineas Quimby and built the Christian Science church; just so Ellen White took the discredited Advent prophecies of William Miller and built the Seventh-Day Adventist church.

But in each case—and this is important to remember—the early distortions and deviations were glossed over with Christian terminology until the delusions were made so attractive that hundreds of thousands of unsuspecting souls have been ensnared and entrapped by their Bible-denying doctrines.

WHY DO SEVENTH-DAY ADVENTISTS OBSERVE SATURDAY AS THE SABBATH?

To a Seventh-Day Adventist, it is a sin to observe the Sabbath on any other day than Saturday. "Because," as one of their official writers states it, "God, in the beginning, set apart the seventh day of creation week as a perpetual memorial of His creative power. Saturday is the seventh day of the week. Sunday is the FIRST day of the week."[5] And as the founder of Seventh-Day Adventism, Mrs. White, states it:

> The sign, or seal, of God is revealed in the observance of the seventh-day Sabbath, the Lord's memorial of creation. . . . The mark of the beast is the opposite of this,— the observance of the first day of the week. This mark distinguishes those who acknowledge the supremacy of the papal authority from those who acknowledge the authority of God.[6]

And in this Mrs. White suggests one of the basic teachings of Seventh-Day Adventists about the Sabbath. For, they say, that since God, in the fourth commandment, lays upon everyone the obligation of remembering "the sabbath day, to keep it holy," and since the Sabbath is the seventh day, it is therefore obligatory upon all who would be Christians to observe Saturday as the Sabbath. Mrs. White even had a vision of the heavenly sanctuary, where she said she saw "Jesus raise the cover of the ark, and she beheld the tables of stone on which the ten commandments were written. She was amazed as she saw the Fourth Commandment in the very centre of the ten precepts, with a soft halo of light encircling it."[7]

Seventh-Day Adventists believe that a Roman Catholic pope and the Emperor Constantine are responsible for changing the Sabbath from Saturday to Sunday. As Mrs. White says:

> I saw that God had not changed the Sabbath, for He never changes. But the pope had changed it from the

seventh to the first day of the week; for he was to change times and laws.[8]

Emperor Constantine, according to Seventh-Day Adventists, made the change in Sabbaths in the year A.D. 321 when he introduced and enforced the observance of the first day of the week as a Christian day of rest. And then in the year A.D. 364, at the Council of Laodicea, the papacy abolished the seventh-day Sabbath in favor of the first day of the week, or Sunday.

The real truth is that neither Constantine nor any Roman pope "changed" the Sabbath from Saturday to Sunday. For Sunday had been observed by Christians from the first Easter Sunday morning as a day of worship and praise. Constantine only gave legal sanction to a practice that was already in effect among Christians. And the Council of Laodicea was not even attended by a Roman pope nor any representative sent by him. The Roman Catholic church had nothing at all to do with the Council of Laodicea, and the Council itself simply regulated some of the long-established customs of the Christians as to their activities on the Lord's day.[9]

That the earliest Christians observed the first day of the week as the Lord's day and the true Christian Sabbath is substantiated by the following testimonies:

Barnabas, the companion of Paul, said in A.D. 60:

> We keep with joyfulness the day in which Christ rose from the dead.

Ignatius, a Jewish Christian, who was led into a saving knowledge of the Lord by St. John the Evangelist, said:

> Every lover of Christ celebrates the Lord's day, consecrated to the resurrection of Christ as the queen and chief of all the days. . . . no longer keeping sabbaths but living according to the Lord's day on which our life has risen again through Him and His death. Let every friend of Christ keep the Lord's day.

Justin Martyr, a convert of Polycarp, who was a convert of St. John, said:

> Sunday is the day on which we all hold our common assembly; Jesus Christ, our Savior on the same day rose from the dead. . . . On the day called Sunday there is a gathering in one place of all who reside within the cities, or in the country places and the memories of the apostles, and the writings of the prophets are read.

Irenaeus in A.D. 167 said:

> On the Lord's day every one of us Christians keep the Sabbath meditating on the law, and rejoicing in the works of God.

Clement wrote in A.D. 192:

> A Christian according to the command of the gospel observes the Lord's day, thereby glorifying the resurrection of the Lord.

For Seventh-Day Adventists then, or for anyone else, to say that it is impossible to be a true Christian and observe the Sabbath on any other day than Saturday is an assertion that cannot be substantiated by either secular or sacred history—in fact, the whole idea that Christians must observe Saturday instead of Sunday is denied most emphatically by both.

God himself makes plain that the Jewish memorial Sabbath was meant for that nation only when He says: "It is a sign between me and the children of Israel for ever" (Exod. 31:17). And like all the other ceremonial practices of Judaism, the Jewish memorial Sabbath was fulfilled by Jesus on the Cross and thus the laws of that Sabbath are not binding on Christians.

As Horton Davies warns: "This doctrine of the Seventh-Day Adventists is an irrelevant legalism in the life of the Spirit."[10] And then he adds Dr. James Black's comment: "To found a church on that ancient, outlived and outdated Jewish Sabbath passes comprehension. There are so many big things worth fighting for. Why fight for a shadow?"[11]

This whole rigid insistence on the observance of Saturday as the Sabbath by the Seventh-Day Adventists is just one more example of how a distortion can be overlayed with religious sentiment and tradition until it becomes, for those who are ensnared by it, a delusion of such dangerous dimension that it can determine destiny.

I. WHAT DO SEVENTH-DAY ADVENTISTS BELIEVE ABOUT CHRIST?

Seventh-Day Adventists believe in the virgin birth of Christ. Their founder, Mrs. Ellen White, however, was apparently inadvertently misleading when she wrote concerning Jesus' brothers that, "being older than Jesus, they felt that He should be under their dictation."[12] Seventh-Day Adventists "explain" that statement by saying that Joseph had sons by a previous marriage.

It is difficult to believe that Seventh-Day Adventists actually believe that Jesus was born with a sinful nature, but that is their clear teaching. Mrs. White, their prophetess, wrote:

> As one of us, He [Jesus] was to give an example of obedience. For this He took upon Himself our nature, and passed through our experiences.[13]

And L. A. Wilcox, writing in their official paper, the *Signs of the Times,* said:

> In His veins was the incubus of a tainted heredity . . . bad blood and inherited meanness.[14]

And in one of the Seventh-Day Adventists' own publications, *Bible Readings for the Home Circle,* there is this statement:

> In His humanity Christ partook of our sinful, fallen nature. If not, then He was not "made like unto His brethren," was not "in all points tempted like as we are," did not overcome as we have to overcome, and is not, therefore, the complete and perfect Saviour man needs and must have to be saved. . . . On His human side, Christ inherited just what every child of Adam inherits—a sinful nature.[15]

But with one short sentence John demolishes this whole structure of blasphemy: "In him is no sin" (John 3:5).

Seventh-Day Adventists deny the finished work of Christ on the Cross. Uriah Smith, for fifty years one of Adventism's most prominent writers, says:

> Christ did not make the atonement when He shed His blood upon the Cross. Let this fact be fixed forever in the mind.[16]

And C. H. Watson, a former president of the Adventist General Conference, said:

> It is impossible to conclude that a complete work of atoning for sin was wrought upon the Cross.[17]

This theory of the incompleteness of Christ's work on the Cross must be more fully discussed under the question about salvation; but in its relation to what the Seventh-Day Adventists believe about Christ, it can be definitely said that Seventh-Day Adventists change the glorious and meaningful words of Christ on the Cross: "It is finished," and make Him say, instead, the insipid and inconclusive words: "To be continued."

II. WHAT DO SEVENTH-DAY ADVENTISTS BELIEVE ABOUT THE BIBLE?

As with all other religious movements which distort the plain teachings of the Bible, the Seventh-Day Adventists come saying, "Yes, we believe the Bible, but our inspired 'Messenger' [or 'prophet,' or 'book'] must be read if the Bible is to be understood." And, here again, it is in the *addition* to the Word of God that the perversions and distortions slip in.

With the Seventh-Day Adventists it is the Bible *and* the writings of their "inspired Messenger," Mrs. Ellen G. White. In the *Review and Herald,* the official organ of the Seventh-Day Adventist church, the editor, F. M. Wilcox, stated:

> As Samuel was a prophet to Israel in his day, as Jeremiah was a prophet to Israel in the days of his captivity, as

John the Baptist came as a special messenger of the Lord to prepare the way for Christ's appearing, so we believe that Mrs. White was a prophet to the church of Christ to-day.[18]

Mr. G. A. Irwin, onetime president of the Adventist General Conference, stated:

The Spirit of Prophecy [meaning the "gift" with which Mrs. White was supposedly endowed] is the only infallible interpreter of Bible principles, since it is Christ through this agency giving the real meaning of His own words.[19]

To take the fantasies of a visionary woman, who was repeatedly "taken up to heaven," where she "saw things," and call those fantasies "inspired" is in itself spiritual folly. But to say that the Bible itself cannot be properly understood without the aid of the neurotic daydreams (termed "hysterical trances" by her own doctor) of a self-deceived "Messenger" is the rankest falsehood of all.

III. WHAT DO SEVENTH-DAY ADVENTISTS BELIEVE ABOUT SALVATION?

Of all the perversions of Seventh-Day Adventism— soul sleep, the observance of Saturday as the Sabbath, the annihilation of the wicked, the weird Advent theories, and the reverence given Mrs. Ellen White—of all these dangerous distortions of historic Christianity, perhaps the most fantastic and Christ-dishonoring and Bible-denying doctrine of Seventh-Day Adventism is its theory of the atonement.

To understand this Adventist theory of the atonement, one must go back to William Miller's prophecy of the second coming of Christ, which, he said, would occur October 22, 1843—later changed to October 22, 1844. When Christ failed to appear on that date, the Adventists were hard pressed for an explanation. Not being as honest as Miller, who renounced the whole thing, Mrs. White and those she was able to gather around her tried to work out a theory as to just what did happen on that October day of 1844.

Mrs. White finally decided, with the aid of a few convenient visions, that what really happened that day in 1844 was that Christ, instead of appearing on earth, had actually finally entered the inner sanctuary, or the "most holy place of the heavenly sanctuary." Mrs. White had, without Biblical substantiation, conceived the idea of two sanctuaries in heaven. Christ, at His ascension, had entered the "first apartment" or outer sanctuary of heaven, and for eighteen hundred years had occupied that outer apartment. Then, all of a sudden, at the end of Daniel's 2,300 days, or years, Christ had entered the "most holy place of the heavenly sanctuary" to "perform the closing work of atonement."

If this seems fanciful and heretical, listen to Mrs. White, the "inspired Messenger," tell it in her own words:

> The sanctuary in heaven, in which Jesus ministers in our behalf, is the great original, of which the sanctuary built by Moses was a copy. The holy places of the sanctuary in heaven are represented by the two apartments in the sanctuary on earth.[20]

> The ministration of the priest, throughout the year in the first apartment of the [earthly] sanctuary, "within the veil" which formed the door and separated the holy place from the outer court, represents the work of ministration upon which Christ entered at His ascension. . . . For eighteen centuries this work of ministration continued in the first apartment of the [heavenly] sanctuary.[21]

> As in the typical service there was a work of atonement at the close of the year so before Christ's work for the redemption of man is completed, there is a work of atonement for the removal of sin from the sanctuary. This is the service which began when the 2300 days ended. At that time, as foretold by Daniel, the prophet, our High Priest entered the most holy. . . . Instead of coming to the earth at the termination of the 2300 days in 1844, Christ then entered the most holy place of the heavenly sanctuary, to perform the closing work of atonement, preparatory to His coming.[22]

Continuing her "explanation" of the significance of 1844, Mrs. White says:

> The work of the investigative judgment and the blotting out of sins is to be accomplished before the second advent of the Lord. Since the dead are to be judged out of the things written in the books, it is impossible that the sins of men should be blotted out until after the judgment at which their cases are to be investigated.
>
> At the time appointed for the judgment—the close of the 2300 days, in 1844—began the work of investigation and blotting out of sins. All who have ever taken upon themselves the name of Christ must pass its searching scrutiny.[23]

So, according to Mrs. White and the Seventh-Day Adventists, it is impossible for anyone to really know his sins are forgiven or blotted out because, according to them, sins will not be actually blotted out until the second advent of Christ. So no one should ever say, "I am saved." For, as Mrs. White said:

> Those who accept Christ, and in their first confidence say, I am saved, are in danger of trusting to themselves. . . . Those who accept the Savior, however sincere their conversion, should never be taught to say or feel that they are saved. This is misleading.[24]

But is it Christ who bears away our sins? No, say the Adventists; it is Satan. Does that sound incredible? Then listen again to Mrs. White, the "Voice" of the Adventists:

> On the day of atonement, two kids of the goats were brought to the door of the tabernacle and lots were cast upon them, "one lot for the Lord, and the other lot for the scapegoat." The goat upon which fell the lot for the Lord, was to be slain as a sin-offering for the people. . . . While the sin-offering pointed to Christ as a sacrifice, and the high priest represented Christ as a mediator, the scapegoat typified Satan, the author of sin, upon whom the sins of the truly penitent will finally be placed. . . . Satan, bearing the guilt of all the sins which he has caused God's people to commit, will be for a thousand years confined to the earth, which will then [during the millennium] be desolate, without inhabitant, and he will at last suffer

the full penalty of sin in the fires that shall destroy all the wicked.[25]

As Dr. Mayer points out:

Whether or not the Adventists realize it, the implication is that the work of man's redemption is not completed by Christ, but actually completed by the devil, a theory which is diametrically opposed to Sacred Scripture and to the glorious person and work of mankind's Redeemer.[26]

What a travesty on the glorious gospel of the grace of God—a gospel that proclaims that one can be saved *now*, and know it: "The Spirit itself beareth witness with our spirit, that we are the children of God" (Rom. 8:16); and a gospel that proclaims that Christ did not die so that He could cleanse some nonexistent sanctuary in heaven—in 1844, or any other time—but that He died to cleanse *human hearts:* "Wherefore Jesus also, that he might sanctify the people with his own blood, suffered without the gate" (Heb. 13:12); and, as we walk in the light, "the blood of Jesus Christ his Son cleanseth us from all sin" (I John 1:7)!

IV. WHAT DO SEVENTH-DAY ADVENTISTS BELIEVE ABOUT THE FUTURE LIFE?

To understand the Adventist theory of the future life, one must first know what Seventh-Day Adventists mean by "soul sleep." And that is a popular phrase for the belief that when a person dies he enters a state of total unconsciousness. As is stated in the Adventist's *Fundamental Principles:*

The state to which we are reduced by death is one of silence, inactivity and entire unconsciousness.[27]

This Adventist theory of soul sleep is further explained in their *Bible Readings for the Home Circle:*

Man does not now possess the undying spiritual nature . . . except as he holds it by faith in Christ; nor will he until the resurrection. Then, if righteous, he will be made immortal, . . . And herein lies a most comforting thought in the Bible doctrine of the sleep of the dead, that in death there is no consciousness. . . . *All* sentient life, animation, activity, thought, and consciousness [cease] at death, and all wait till the resurrection for their future life and eternal rewards.[28]

Seventh-Day Adventists believe that those who have died are neither in a state of happiness nor in a state of condemnation—they are in a state of total unconsciousness; their souls are sleeping in the grave. But the scripture texts used to "substantiate" this theory are always those which refer to the body and never to the spirit. And the many scriptures that deny this doctrine of soul sleep, the Adventists evade and twist and distort—as, for example, the scriptural teaching that the thief on the cross entered paradise immediately upon dying. The Adventists get around this, as do the Jehovah's Witnesses, by changing the punctuation so that it reads, "Verily, I say unto thee today: Thou, etc."; instead of the way Luke records it: "Verily, I say unto thee, To day shalt thou, etc."

This theory of soul sleep is, of course, another outgrowth of the Adventist doctrine of conditional immortality—the idea that only those who are found righteous at the final judgment will be granted immortality. As Mrs. White expresses it:

Upon the fundamental error of natural immortality rests the doctrine of consciousness in death, a doctrine like eternal torment, opposed to the teaching of the Scriptures, to the dictates of reason and to our feelings of humanity.[29]

Man, according to the Seventh-Day Adventists, is not immortal; he only has the right to *earn* immortality by a righteous life. And if he is judged righteous in the final judgment, he will then have immortality "conferred" upon him.

But this whole theory of soul sleep is contradicted emphatically by the New Testament in the story of

Lazarus (Luke 16:22-25), in the promise of Christ to the thief on the cross (Luke 23:43), in the wail of the martyrs (Rev. 6:9-11), and in the ministry of Christ's spirit to the departed between His own death and resurrection (I Pet. 3:19; 4:6).

AND WHAT HAPPENS TO THE WICKED?

They are annihilated—completely destroyed. There is no eternal punishment in Seventh-Day Adventist doctrine. As Mrs. White said: "The theory of eternal punishment is one of the false doctrines that constitute the wine of the abominations of Babylon."[30] Wicked men and Satan himself are all to be utterly destroyed by fire.

In the Adventist book *Bible Readings for the Home Circle,* this is emphatically stated:

> The wicked are to be utterly destroyed—consumed away into smoke, brought to ashes. . . . Their destruction will, in fact, be an act of love and mercy on the part of God; for to perpetuate their lives would only be to perpetuate sin, sorrow, suffering, and misery. . . . This fire is called "everlasting" because of the character of the work it does; just as it is called "unquenchable" because it cannot be put out, and not because it will not go out when it has done its work.[31]

The Seventh-Day Adventists do not believe in hell as the Bible teaches it, and to say that the wicked are annihilated, completely destroyed, is to deny the Bible, which says: "The smoke of their torment ascendeth up for ever and ever" (Rev. 14:11). And to deny eternal punishment is to deny the emphatic statement of Jesus: "These shall go away into everlasting punishment: but the righteous into life eternal" (Matt. 25:46). Notice, Jesus did not say "everlasting annihilation," but "everlasting punishment."

According to Jesus, "everlasting" punishment is to be just as "everlasting" for the wicked as the bliss of heaven is to be "everlasting" for the righteous. And to deny one is to deny both.

WITH SUCH DOCTRINES, DO THE SEVENTH-DAY ADVENTISTS ACCOMPLISH ANY GOOD?

Indeed they do. Their missionary dedication, their medical work, and their educational emphasis are all highly commendable. And their facility with the Bible is a reflection upon those members of churches which profess to be "Bible-centered" and yet enjoy their Bible so little and use their Bible so ineffectively.

The zeal with which Seventh-Day Adventists advance their teaching is also as commendable as the results of that zeal are deplorable. For one can admire the earnestness and sincerity of the zealous and at the same time deplore the errors and darkness into which that zeal leads others.

With such zeal and earnestness, the Seventh-Day Adventists have developed an activity that is, as Dr. Mayer points out, "out of proportion to their numerical strength."[32] When one considers that infants and children are not included in the Seventh-Day Adventist membership rolls, and then remembers that there are now over one million Seventh-Day Adventists around the world, with 275,733 members in the United States organized into 3,016 churches, and yet with this comparatively small membership they are able to have 42 publishing houses distributed over the world, with 6 in the United States, with literature printed in 198 languages and dialects, and in Braille for the blind; and that they have 3 junior colleges, 11 liberal arts colleges, and 2 graduate schools—a medical and dental school and a theological seminary; and that they support hundreds of secondary and elementary schools; and that they now have 1,050 radio broadcasts weekly; and that over 2,000,-000 students have enrolled in their Bible correspondence schools, and have an international broadcast, "The Voice of Prophecy," that goes out over 856 stations in 15 languages and 52 countries, and a television program, "Faith for Today," that is released weekly over 108 outlets[33]— when one considers all their activities around the world and knows that many Adventists pay a double tithe—one for the local church work and the other for the church at large—and sees them as decent neighbors and dedicated church members, and knows that in spite of their distorted doctrines many of them are sincere Christians, one can but admire them, as persons, even though one must at the same time reject the strange, perverted, and bizarre beliefs of their church.

Why, then, am I not a Seventh-Day Adventist?

1. I am not a Seventh-Day Adventist because, as a Nazarene, I believe that Jesus Christ was holy—sinless—

And the Word was made flesh, and dwelt among us, (and we beheld his glory, the glory as of the only begotten of the Father,) full of grace and truth (John 1:14),

and so I could never believe in the Seventh-Day Adventist Christ, who "inherited a sinful nature."

2. I am not a Seventh-Day Adventist because, as a Nazarene, I believe that Jesus Christ paid the full price for man's redemption on the Cross—

For Christ also hath once suffered for sins, the just for the unjust, that he might bring us to God, being put to death in the flesh, but quickened by the Spirit (I Pet. 3:18),

and so I could never believe in the Seventh-Day Adventist Christ, who made an "incomplete atonement" on Calvary, and will one day share with Satan the blotting out of my sins.

3. I am not a Seventh-Day Adventist because, as a Nazarene, I believe that Jesus Christ by His death on the Cross makes it possible for me to know here and now that I am saved and sanctified—

There is therefore now no condemnation to them which are in Christ Jesus, who walk not after the flesh, but after the Spirit (Rom. 8:1),

and,

The Spirit itself beareth witness with our spirit, that we are the children of God (Rom. 8:16),

and,

If we walk in the light, as he is in the light, we have fellowship one with another, and the blood of Jesus Christ his Son cleanseth us from all sin (I John 1:7),

and so I could never believe in the Seventh-Day Adventist practice of postponing until the Second Coming what Christ offers one today.

4. I am not a Seventh-Day Adventist because, as a Nazarene, I believe that when Christ ascended into heaven He did not enter an outer sanctuary or apartment, but went straight into the presence of His Father—

Neither by the blood of goats and calves, but by his own blood he entered in once into the holy place, having obtained eternal redemption for us (Heb. 9:12),

and,

But this man, after he had offered one sacrifice for sins for ever, sat down on the right hand of God; from henceforth expecting till his enemies be made his footstool. For by one offering he hath perfected for ever them that are sanctified. Whereof the Holy Ghost also is a witness to us (Heb. 10:12-15),

and so I could never believe in the Seventh-Day Adventist Christ, who for eighteen hundred years waited around in the anteroom of heaven until, in 1844, He finally entered "the most holy place."

5. I am not a Seventh-Day Adventist because, as a Nazarene, I believe that the Bible, interpreted by the Holy Spirit, is a sufficient guide from earth to heaven—

The Holy Spirit Whom the Father will send in My name, will be your teacher and will bring to your minds all that I have said to you (John 14:26, Phillips),

and so I could never believe in the Seventh-Day Adventist Bible, that must be "interpreted" and "explained" by Mrs. White before it is a trustworthy lamp lighting the way from earth to heaven.

6. I am not a Seventh-Day Adventist because, as a Nazarene, I believe that the souls of the dead are in a state of bliss or a state of condemnation—

And Jesus said unto him, Verily I say unto thee, To day shalt thou be with me in paradise (Luke 23:43),
and,

And it came to pass, that the beggar died, and was carried by the angels into Abraham's bosom: the rich man also died, and was buried; and in hell he lift up his eyes, being in torments, and seeth Abraham afar off, and Lazarus in his bosom (Luke 16:22-23),

and so I could never believe in the Seventh-Day Adventist heresy of soul sleep, or that the dead are unconscious.

7. I am not a Seventh-Day Adventist because, as a Nazarene, I believe in the reality of everlasting punishment for the wicked—

And he cried and said, Father Abraham, have mercy on me, and send Lazarus, that he may dip the tip of his finger in water, and cool my tongue; for I am tormented in this flame. But Abraham said, Son, remember that thou in thy lifetime receivedst thy good things, and likewise Lazarus evil things: but now he is comforted, and thou art tormented. And beside all this, between us and you there is a great gulf fixed: so that they which would pass from hence to you cannot; neither can they pass to us that would come from thence (Luke 16:24-26), and so I could never believe the Seventh-Day Adventist teaching that the wicked are annihilated—completely destroyed, along with Satan, in fire that will one day be quenched.

8. I am not a Seventh-Day Adventist because, as a Nazarene, I believe in the immortality of every human soul—

And these shall go away into everlasting punishment: but the righteous into life eternal (Matt. 25:46),

and so I could never believe the Seventh-Day Adventist doctrine of conditional immortality—that only the righteous will have immortality bestowed upon them.

9. I am not a Seventh-Day Adventist because, as a Nazarene, I believe that no man knows or can know the exact time of the second coming of Christ—

But of that day and that hour knoweth no man, no, not the angels which are in heaven, neither the Son, but the Father. Take ye heed, watch and pray: for ye know not when the time is (Mark 13:32-33),

and so I could never believe the Adventist theory or practice of setting dates for the Second Advent, which they have done from William Miller's repudiated prophecy on.

10. I am not a Seventh-Day Adventist because, as a Nazarene, I believe in the Christian Sabbath, which is the Lord's day—

And upon the first day of the week, when the disciples came together to break bread, Paul preached unto them, ready to depart on the morrow; and continued his speech until midnight (Acts 20:7),

and so I could never believe that the Seventh-Day Adventist Jewish memorial Sabbath is still obligatory upon Christians. True Christians since the resurrection of Christ have observed the Lord's day, or the first day of the week, as the Christian Sabbath. That particular law was nailed to the Cross, was nullified by Christ's death, and hence is no longer obligatory for those who are walking in the spirit of the grace of the gospel, and not according to the letter of a dead law.

Don't trust every spirit, dear friends of mine, but test them to discover whether they come from God or not. For the world is full of false prophets.

—I John 4:1 (Phillips)

Conclusion

Although the Mormons, the Jehovah's Witnesses, the Christian Scientists, the Seventh-Day Adventists, and the Roman Catholics have their own distinguishing differences they all have at least four dangerous distortions in common:

1. THEY ALL DENY THE ADEQUACY OF JESUS CHRIST. The thin veneer of idealism soon cracks and the real Christ of the cults and the Roman Catholics appears— but it is not the Christ the Bible portrays. To the Mormon, Christ is the Son of Adam-God and Mary—*not* conceived by the Holy Ghost. To the Jehovah's Witness, Christ is a good man, a "messenger" from God who is now dead—"forever dead." To the Christian Scientist, Christ is not God's Son, but only an "idea," and exists only as an "influence" to further divine science. To the Seventh-Day Adventist, Christ shares with Satan the task of blotting out men's sins, thus making His cry, "It is finished," an absurdity. To the Roman Catholic, Christ's importance is overshadowed by the Virgin Mary, for the whole "cult of Mary" is based upon the Christ-dishonoring belief that Mary is more merciful than her Son.

How subtle and clever—to use Christ's name as a convenient "come-on" to those who want to believe, and then to dishonor and discredit Him by denying His deity, by nullifying His redemptive purpose and power, or by replacing Him with His mother, Mary, by giving to her, a mere mortal, that worship and devotion and intensity

131

of love that rightfully belong only to Jesus Christ, the Son of God!

2. THEY ALL DENY THE ADEQUACY OF THE BIBLE. Each in its turn comes, saying, "The Bible—*and* our book." With the Mormons it is, "The Bible—*and* the *Book of Mormon.*" With the Jehovah's Witnesses it is, "The Bible —*and* Pastor Russell's *Scripture Studies*"; or, "The Bible —*and* our *New World Translation.*" With the Christian Scientists it is, "The Bible—*and* Mrs. Eddy's *Science and Health with Key to the Scriptures.*" With the Seventh-Day Adventists it is, "The Bible—*and* the 'inspired' writings of Mrs. White, their 'Messenger.'" With the Roman Catholics it is, "The Bible—*and* the *traditions* of the Roman Catholic church."

The self-styled "prophets" of the cults invariably claim, in their own "inspired" way, the same authority to "supplement" the Bible with their teachings and "revelations" as do the "infallible" popes of the Roman Catholic church in their dogmas and decrees.

3. THEY ALL ULTIMATELY DENY THAT SALVATION IS BY FAITH. To the cultists, and to Roman Catholics, salvation is by works—not by faith. To the Mormon, salvation is attained by obedience to the rules as administered and interpreted by the "priesthood" of the Mormon church. To the Jehovah's Witness, salvation consists of being "imitators" of Jesus in "witnessing" to that Kingdom. To the Christian Scientist, salvation is "demonstrating" that sin is "error, an illusion of material sense." To a Seventh-Day Adventist, salvation is a matter of observing Saturday as the Sabbath, and hoping that when Christ appears He will lay the sins of those who have been faithful upon Satan, who will bear them away. To a Roman Catholic, salvation is gained by the observance of the sacraments and regulations of the Roman Catholic church, and whatever grace a Roman Catholic obtains

must be obtained through intermediaries—the church, the priests, the Virgin Mary, and the saints.

One of the most common characteristics of distorted religious belief is this emphasis upon salvation by works instead of salvation by faith. It is Bible-denying because it contradicts the clear and unequivocal teaching of God's Word. It is Christ-dishonoring because it denies the finished work of Christ upon the Cross.

It is a periodic necessity, it seems, for someone to slash through the enveloping religious red tape and the encroaching fetters of religious organization, and to cry out to the multitudes who sincerely hunger and pray for salvation: *"The just shall live by faith."*

4. THEY ALL DENY THE BIBLE TEACHING ON THE FUTURE LIFE. To the Mormon, heaven is a place where the "exalted," those who have contracted "celestial" marriage in a Mormon temple, will have children and will eventually become "gods," while hell will be suffered by only a few—"less than the number of fingers on one hand." To a Jehovah's Witness, heaven will be populated by only 144,000 of the most faithful "Witnesses," while the rest of the "good" Witnesses will inhabit earth forever. And hell, to a Jehovah's Witness, is nonexistent—the wicked are annihilated. To a Christian Scientist, heaven and hell are states of mind, for "the sinner makes his own hell by doing evil, and the saint his own heaven by doing right." To a Seventh-Day Adventist, death is immediately followed by "soul sleep"; and then, at the second advent of Christ, immortality will be bestowed upon the righteous, while the wicked, along with Satan, will be absolutely annihilated. To the Roman Catholic, death is followed by purgatory for everyone, but the faithful Roman Catholic will not suffer there as long as the wicked, or willful non-Catholics; and ultimately, everyone will go to heaven, except the willfully disobedient.

All true Christians must be ever alert and on their guard against *anyone* who comes saying, as Marcus Bach's Mormon friend said of his religion: "It's Christianity *plus.*"

For it is out of that treacherous and poisonous *"plus"* that have flowed all the distortions, the deviations, the blasphemies, the heresies, and the whole array of false doctrines that have plagued Christianity through the centuries and today pervert the faith of millions. These, then, are the dominant distortions which have emerged as each group represented in this study has faced the light of "Thus saith the Lord," and answered the four pivotal questions concerning Christ, the Bible, salvation, and the future life.

One can only hope that even this brief but honest glance at these distortions will prove helpful to those who are called upon to give a reason for their faith, and who sincerely desire to be able to knowingly say, "I am *this,* and not *that*"—and to say it in a tone of Christian charity but with the firm and abiding conviction of Christian certainty.

It is only those who are *sure* of Christ—His deity, His redemptive love, His forgiving and cleansing power—who are safe from those who would ensnare by the clever disguises of their Christ-dishonoring doctrines.

It is only those who are *sure* of the Bible—its inspiration, its authority, and its adequacy—who are safe from those who would entrap by their cunningly devised, but Bible-denying, fables.

It is only those who are *sure* of salvation—the certain assurance through the Holy Spirit of God's pardoning and purifying power—who are safe from the deceits and delusions of those who substitute works for faith.

It is only those who are *sure* of their "hope of glory" who are safe from the warped and twisted perversions of those who reject the idea of hell and restrict heaven to the exclusive enjoyment of their own ecclesiastical elect.

May God help us then, as Christians, and as Nazarenes, to be so *sure*, so humbly and so gratefully *sure*, that we will not only be witnesses *against* the distortions and the deviations and the delusions of those who would deceive, but that we will be effective witnesses *to* the *truth*—to the truth as it is revealed in Christ, as it is reported in the Bible, as it is realized in experience, and as it will be rewarded in the life to come.

And in this way, and only in this way, will we be able to be true to the mission and the message of *holiness evangelism,* which is our own sacred heritage and our one surest hope.

	NAZARENE	MORMON	ROMAN CATHOLIC
Christ	Born of Virgin Mary. Died on the Cross to redeem mankind. Arose from the dead. Ascended into heaven. Now making intercession at right hand of God. Will come again in like manner as He went away. Eternally one with the Father.	Jesus is the son of Adam-God and Mary. Not conceived by the Holy Ghost. When He returns, He will establish two cities as headquarters: Jerusalem and Independence, Missouri, where He will administer affairs of the "Theocracy."	Believe in the deity of Christ. Believe that through His merit, His sacrifice, His love, the way is open from earth to heaven. Mary almost replaces Christ in devotion and commitment, until real Christ is obscured.
Bible	It is the Word of God. Contains all truth necessary to faith and Christian living. Whatever is not contained in Bible is not to be enjoined as an article of faith.	Believe the Bible is the Word of God "as far as it is translated correctly." Supplement the Bible with the *Book of Mormon*, which is "equally inspired." Theory of progressive revelation denies the sufficiency and finality of the Bible.	Bible is God's word to man—but it must be interpreted by "infallible" Catholic church. Bible is still a "dark" book to most Catholics. In America, Catholics encouraged to read "their" versions of Bible; in non-Protestant countries, Bible is still an unknown Book.
Salvation	Sin is twofold: acts or purposes of transgressions, and corrupted nature. Christ made full atonement for sin, which atonement is only ground of salvation. Justification is by faith, preceded by repentance. Entire sanctification is act of God freeing heart from original sin and filling with power.	Must work out salvation by obedience to rules and ordinances of Mormon church. Baptism is for remission of sins. Vicarious baptism for the dead by living Mormons—which rite is always performed in Mormon Temple.	Original sin is washed away in water baptism. Salvation by observance of sacraments of Roman Catholic church. No direct access to God —grace must be mediated through priest, church, Mary, saints. Those knowingly outside Roman Catholic church will be lost.
Future Life	The bodies of the just and the unjust shall be raised to life and united with their spirits. Everlasting life in heaven for all who savingly believe in and obediently follow Christ. The finally impenitent shall suffer eternally in hell.	Mormons accept immortality of man. Those Mormons married for eternity will be "exalted" and will eventually rise to "godhood"—having offspring through eternity. Sinners to have second chance after death, but those few "sons of perdition" will suffer eternally in hell.	Everyone at death goes to purgatory—a place of punishment for sins. Length of stay in purgatory varies. The faithful eventually experience supernatural happiness in heaven. Demons, the unbaptized and willfully evil will be punished eternally for their sins.

JEHOVAH'S WITNESS	CHRISTIAN SCIENTIST	SEVENTH-DAY ADVENTIST
Deny the deity of Christ. His human existence ended on the Cross, and He is dead —"forever dead." No one knows what became of His body. Christ was only a messenger, an angel, a created being, a perfect man, a representative of God, but not God-Man.	Deny the deity of Christ. Christ is only a divine "idea." Deny the Virgin Birth. Christ's "seeming" death was only a "misunderstanding." Deny His second coming— saying that the Second Coming is only the "advancing idea of God in Christian Science." Christ is only the "Way-Shower."	Jesus was born with a sinful nature. Deny the finished work of Christ on the Cross by saying that He did not enter the inner "sanctuary" of heaven until 1844. Christ is coming back to earth again—and soon.
Read it and memorize it and quote it—out of context, and thus "wrest" the Scriptures. Refuse to take the Bible "as is," and insist that Russell's interpretations and the *New World Translations* are necessary if the Bible is to be understood.	Profess great respect for the Bible but deny its teachings, its finality, and its gospel. Bible is inadequate and must be interpreted by Mrs. Eddy's *Science and Health*. Believe Mrs. Eddy's writings are "inspired," and necessary to the understanding of the Bible.	Believe the Bible is the Word of God, but also believe Mrs. White's writings "inspired," and her writings must be read along with the Bible if the Bible is to be understood. Mrs. White is the "Voice," the "Messenger" of God interpreting the Bible to the people of this age.
Salvation consists of being "imitators" of Jesus in being "witnesses" to Jehovah God. Know nothing of conversion or cleansing. It is salvation by works, and not by faith. Salvation is only for those who are faithful Witnesses.	Man is incapable of sin, for sin is unreal, an error, an illusion of mortal mind. Salvation is "demonstrating" the unreality of sin. No need for a Saviour, as sin is destroyed by the demonstration of it as error. No redemptive power or purpose in the cross of Christ. Man can free himself through the practice of "divine" Science.	No one should ever say he is saved—for no one knows that, and will not know it until Christ returns to earth. Christ casts sins upon Satan, who will one day bear them away to destruction. No cleansing of the human heart—Christ cleanses the "inner sanctuary" of heaven —since 1844.
Death is cessation of being—destruction, complete and total. All who die will be "restored" at the second coming of Christ and will be given a second chance. Those who persist in their rejection will be annihilated, for there is no hell—no place of eternal torment. 144,000 "special" Witnesses will be in heaven; other "Witnesses" will be on earth.	Death is an illusion—it is unreal. There is no heaven and no hell in a geographical sense —they are merely states of mind—heaven being a "harmonious" state and hell being "mortal belief, error, remorse, self-destruction."	At death the soul sleeps, enters a state of entire unconsciousness. Only those who at the judgment are found righteous will have immortality conferred upon them. The wicked are annihilated —completely destroyed, utterly consumed, brought to ashes. Hell itself will be destroyed along with the wicked.

Notes

PREFACE

1. George A. Buttrick, *So We Believe, So We Pray* (New York and Nashville: Abingdon-Cokesbury Press, 1951), pp. 17-18.
2. Whittaker Chambers, *Witness* (New York: Random House, 1952), p. 5.

CHAPTER I

1. Church of the Nazarene, *Manual* (Kansas City, Missouri: Nazarene Publishing House, 1956), p. 28.
2. *Ibid.,* p. 32.
3. *Ibid.,* p. 3.
4. *Ibid.,* pp. 28-29.
5. *Ibid.,* p. 29.
6. *Ibid.,* p. 30.
7. *Ibid.,* p. 31.
8. *Ibid.,* pp. 31-32.
9. *Ibid.,* pp. 32-33.
10. James B. Chapman, *Nazarene Primer* (Kansas City, Missouri: Nazarene Publishing House, 1949), p. 59.
11. William Warren Sweet, *American Culture and Religion* (Dallas, Texas: Southern Methodist University Press, 1951), p. 90.
12. *Ibid.,* p. 98.

CHAPTER II

1. Leo Rosten, *A Guide to the Religions of America* (New York: Simon and Schuster, 1955), p. 91.
2. Gordon B. Hinckley, *What of the Mormons?* (Salt Lake City: The Church of the Latter-day Saints, 1947), p. 9.
3. Ernest Sutherland Bates, *American Faith* (New York: W. W. Norton Co., 1940), p. 344.
4. *Ibid.,* p. 354.
5. W. E. Biederwolf, *Mormonism Under the Searchlight* (Grand Rapids: Eerdmans Publishing Co., 1956), p. 20.
6. Horton Davies, *Christian Deviations* (New York: Philosophical Library, Inc., 1954), pp. 74-75.
7. Bates, *op. cit.,* p. 346.
8. Rosten, *op. cit.,* p. 92.
9. Joseph Fielding Smith, *The Way to Perfection* (Salt Lake City, Utah: Deseret News Press, 1953), p. 233.

10. F. E. Mayer, *The Religious Bodies of America* (St. Louis, Missouri: Concordia Publishing House, 1954), p. 454.

11. Joseph Fielding Smith, *op. cit.*, p. 322.

12. Rosten, *op. cit.*, p. 93.

13. Brigham Young, *Discourses* (Salt Lake City, Utah: The Church of Jesus Christ of Latter-day Saints), I, 50-51.

14. James E. Talmage, *The Articles of Faith* (Salt Lake City, Utah: The Church of Jesus Christ of Latter-day Saints, 1952), p. 2.

15. Talmage, *op. cit.*, p. 2.

16. Joseph Fielding Smith, *op. cit.*, p. 334.

17. Talmage, *op. cit.*, p. 2.

18. Hinckley, *op. cit.*, pp. 26-27.

19. Rosten, *op. cit.*, p. 95.

20. Hinckley, *op. cit.*, pp. 23-24.

21. Rosten, *op. cit.*, p. 95.

22. Braden, *These Also Believe* (New York: The Macmillan Co., 1949), p. 448.

23. *Book of Mormon* (1921 ed.; Salt Lake City: The Church of Jesus Christ of Latter-day Saints), p. 296.

24. Joseph Fielding Smith, *op. cit.*, p. 304

25. *Ibid.*, pp. 8-9.

26. Frank S. Mead, *Handbook of Denominations in the United States* (New York and Nashville: Abingdon Press, 1956), p. 126.

27. *Ibid.*, p. 126.

CHAPTER III

1. W. C. Irvine, *Heresies Exposed* (New York: Loizeaux Brothers, 1956), p. 147.

2. Joseph Zacchello, *Ins and Outs of Romanism* (New York: Loizeaux Brothers, 1956), p. 26.

3. James Hasting Nichols, *Primer for Protestants* (New York: Association Press, 1949), p. 64.

4. James Cardinal Gibbons, *The Faith of Our Fathers* (New York: P. J. Kennedy and Sons, 1917), pp. 155-56.

5. Joseph Zacchello, *op. cit.*

6. Irvine, *op. cit.*, pp. 142-43.

7. J. Paul Williams, *What Americans Believe and How They Worship* (New York: Harper and Brothers, 1952), p. 31.

8. Zacchello, *op. cit.*, p. 117.

9. Williams, *op. cit.*, pp. 35-37.

10. *Ibid.*, p. 37.

11. Harrison and Wilson, *How to Win Souls* (Wheaton, Illinois: Scripture Press, 1952), p. 113.

12. F. E. Mayer, *op. cit.*, p. 39.

13. Harrison and Wilson, *op. cit.*, pp. 111-16.

14. Williams, *op. cit.*, p. 34.

CHAPTER IV

1. Marley Cole, *Jehovah's Witnesses* (New York: Vantage Press, 1955), p. 17.

2. *Ibid.*, p. 101.

3 *The Watchtower* (Brooklyn, New York: Watchtower Bible and Tract Society), October 1, 1931.

4. H. H. Stroup, *The Jehovah's Witnesses* (New York: Columbia University Press, 1945), pp. 12-13.

5. Cole, *op. cit.*, p. 51.

6. Walter R. Martin and Norman H. Klann, *Jehovah of the Watchtower* (Grand Rapids, Michigan: Zondervan, 1956), p. 27.

7. Marcus Bach, *They Have Found a Faith* (Indianapolis and New York: The Bobbs-Merrill Co., 1946), pp. 25-26.

8. Rutherford, *Theocracy* (Brooklyn, New York: Watchtower Bible and Tract Society, 1944), p. 18.

9. *Religion Reaps the Whirlwind* (Brooklyn, New York: Watchtower Bible and Tract Society, 1944), pp. 58-59.

10. Rutherford, *Deliverance* (Brooklyn, New York: Watchtower Bible and Tract Society), p. 222.

11. *Let God Be True* (Brooklyn, New York: Watchtower Bible and Tract Society, 1946), pp. 234-36.

12. Russell, *The Divine Plan of the Ages* (Brooklyn, New York: Watchtower Bible and Tract Society), I, 179.

13. Russell, *Studies in the Scriptures* (Brooklyn, New York: Watchtower Bible and Tract Society), Vol. 1.

14. *Ibid.*, I, 84.

15. *Reconciliation* (Brooklyn, New York: Watchtower Bible and Tract Society), p. 113.

16. *Let God Be True*, p. 88.

17. *Ibid.*, p. 91.

18. Rutherford, *The Harp of God* (Brooklyn, New York: Watchtower Bible and Tract Society), p. 99.

19. *Ibid.*, pp. 101, 128.

20. Russell, *op. cit.*, II, 129.

21. *Ibid.*, I, 231.

22. *Ibid.*, V, 453-54.

23. Rutherford, *op. cit.*, p. 170.

24. Luke 24:36-43.

25. Russell, *The Time Is at Hand* (Brooklyn, New York: Watchtower Bible and Tract Society), II, 107.

26. The *Watchtower*, September 15, 1910, p. 298.

27. Martin and Klann, *op. cit.*, p. 161.

28. II Peter 3:16.

29. Russell, *Studies in the Scriptures*, I, 150.

30. *Ibid.*, V, 169.

31. *Ibid.*, p. 210.

32. *Ibid.*, p. 329.

33. *Ibid.*, p. 362.

34. Rutherford, *op. cit.*, pp. 45-46.

35. Rutherford, *Riches* (Brooklyn, New York: Watchtower Bible and Tract Society), p. 183.

36. Luke 23:43.

37. Russell, *Hell, What Is It?* (Brooklyn, New York: Watchtower Bible and Tract Society).

38. Russell, *Studies in the Scriptures*, I, 128.

39. Rutherford, *Creation* (Brooklyn, New York: Watchtower Bible and Tract Society), p. 256.

40. *Let God Be True*, pp. 72-73.

41. *Ibid.*, p. 79.

42. *Ibid.*, p. 80.

43. Leo Rosten, *A Guide to the Religions of America* (New York: Simon and Schuster, 1955), p. 61.

44. *Let God Be True*, p. 79.

45. Cole, *op. cit.*, pp. 78-79.

46. Rosten, *op. cit.*, p. 161.

47. *Ibid.*, p. 59.

48. *Ibid.*, p. 64.

49. Cole, *op. cit.*, p. 17.

50. *Ibid.*, p. 25.

51. Frank S. Mead, *Handbook of Denominations in the United States* (New York and Nashville: Abingdon Press, 1956), p. 118.

52. Richard Harris, *New Yorker Magazine*, June 16, 1956, p. 72.

53. Mead, *op. cit.*, p. 116.

54. Harris, *op. cit.*, p. 74.

55. Mead, *op. cit.*, p. 116.

56. Harris, *op. cit.*, pp. 74, 92.

57. Horton Davies, *Christian Deviations* (New York: Philosophical Library, Inc., 1954), p. 66.

CHAPTER V

1. Leo Rosten, *A Guide to the Religions of America* (New York: Simon and Schuster, 1955), p. 21.

2. Horton Davies, *Christian Deviations* (New York: Philosophical Library, Inc., 1954), p. 32.

3. *Ibid.*, p. 32.

4. Rosten, *op. cit.*, p. 22.

5. Mary Baker Eddy, *Science and Health with Key to the Scriptures* (1934 ed.; Boston, Massachusetts: Christian Science Publishing Society), p. 361.

6. *Ibid.,* p. 29.

7. Mary Baker Eddy, *Autobiography* (Boston, Massachusetts: Christian Science Publishing Society), p. 96.

8. F. E. Mayer, *The Religious Bodies of America* (St. Louis, Missouri: Concordia Publishing House, 1954), pp. 526-27.

9. Rosten, *op. cit.,* pp. 22-23.

10. Mary Baker Eddy, *Christian Science Journal,* January, 1901.

11. Mary Baker Eddy, *Miscellaneous Writings* (1934 ed.; Boston, Massachusetts: Christian Science Publishing Society), p. 331.

12. Rosten, *op. cit.,* pp. 28-29.

13. Eddy, *Science and Health with Key to the Scriptures,* p. 339.

14. *Ibid.,* pp. 23-25.

15. Rosten, *op. cit.,* p. 28.

16. Eddy, *op. cit.,* p. 291.

17. *Ibid.,* p. 588.

18. *Ibid.,* pp. 12-13.

19. Mayer, *op. cit.,* p. 532.

20. Eddy, *op. cit.,* pp. 16-17.

21. *Ibid.,* p. 55.

22. *Ibid.,* pp. 46-47.

23. *Ibid.,* p. 331.

24. Frank S. Mead, *Handbook of Denominations in the United States* (New York and Nashville: Abingdon Press, 1956), p. 61.

25. *Ibid.,* p. 62.

CHAPTER VI

1. Horton Davies, *Christian Deviations* (New York: Philosophical Library, Inc., 1954), p. 55.

2. Stanley I. Stuber, *How We Got Our Denominations* (New York: Association Press, 1948), p. 205.

3. Vergilius Ferm, *The American Church* (New York: Philosophical Library, Inc., 1953), p. 375.

4. Dumas Malone, *Dictionary of American Biography* (New York: Charles Scribner's and Sons, 1936), Vol. 20, p. 98.

5. Leo Rosten, *A Guide to the Religions of America* (New York: Simon and Schuster, 1955), p. 134.

6. Ellen White, *Testimonies for the Church* (Takoma Park, Washington, D.C.: White Publications), VIII, 117.

7. W. C. Irvine, *Heresies Exposed* (New York: Loizeaux Brothers, Inc., 1955), pp. 162-63.

8. Jones, E. B., *Why You Should Not Be a Seventh-Day Adventist* (Minneapolis, Minnesota: Guardians of the Faith, 1949), p. 42.

9. Jones, *op. cit.*, p. 44.

10. Davies, *op. cit.*, p. 59.

11. *Ibid.*, p. 60.

12. Ellen White, *The Desire of Ages* (1898 ed.; Takoma Park, Washington, D.C.; White Publications), pp. 86-87.

13. *Ibid.*, p. 24.

14. Jones, *op. cit.*, p. 6.

15. Irvine, *op. cit.*, p. 159.

16. Jones, *op. cit.*, p. 9.

17. *Ibid.*, p. 9.

18. *Ibid.*, p. 54.

19. *Ibid.*, p. 54.

20. Ellen White, *The Great Controversy* (Takoma Park, Washington, D.C.: White Publications), p. 414.

21. *Ibid.*, pp. 420-21.

22. *Ibid.*, pp. 421-22.

23. *Ibid.*, pp. 485-86.

24. Ellen White, *Christ's Object Lessons* (Takoma Park, Washington, D.C.: White Publications), p. 155.

25. White, *The Great Controversy* (1911 ed.), pp. 419, 422, 485-86.

26. F. E. Mayer, *The Religious Bodies of America* (St. Louis, Missouri: Concordia Publishing House, 1954), p. 439.

27. Ellen White, *Fundamental Principles* (Takoma Park, Washington, D.C.: White Publications), p. 12.

28. Jones, *op. cit.*, pp. 18-19.

29. Irvine, *op. cit.*, p. 162.

30. *Ibid.*

31. Jones, *op. cit.*, p. 21.

32. Mayer, *op. cit.*, p. 433.

33. Frank S. Mead, *Handbook of Denominations in the United States* (New York and Nashville: Abingdon Press, 1956), p. 18.

Date Due

AUG 28 '85			
DEC 27 '87			
FEB 13 '91			
NOV 24 '96			

Code 4386-04, CLS-4, Broadman Supplies, Nashville, Tenn.,
Printed in U.S.A.